FOREIGN POLICY OF THE UNITED STATES

DIPLOMATIC IMMUNITY: PRIVILEGES AND ABUSES

FOREIGN POLICY OF THE UNITED STATES

Additional books in this series can be found on Nova's website under the Series tab.

Additional E-books in this series can be found on Nova's website under the E-books tab.

FOREIGN POLICY OF THE UNITED STATES

DIPLOMATIC IMMUNITY: PRIVILEGES AND ABUSES

JONATHAN G. CARTER
EDITOR

Nova Science Publishers, Inc.
New York

For permission to use material from this book please contact us:
Telephone 631-231-7269; Fax 631-231-8175
Web Site: http://www.novapublishers.com

Library of Congress Cataloging-in-Publication Data

Diplomatic immunity : privileges and abuses / editors, Jonathan G. Carter.
p. cm.
Includes index.
ISBN 978-1-61324-706-8 (softcover)
1. Diplomatic privileges and immunities--United States. 2. Diplomatic privileges and immunities. 3. Household employees--Abuse of--Prevention. I. Carter, Jonathan G.
KF5113.D57 2011
342.73'0412--dc23

2011016743

Published by Nova Science Publishers, Inc. † New York

CONTENTS

PREFACE

To conduct foreign relations and promote the interest of their nationals located abroad, diplomatic and consular officers must be free to represent their respective states without hindrance by their hosts. Recognizing this, states receiving foreign diplomats and consular officers have long accorded such persons with certain privileges and immunities on the basis of comity, reciprocity and international agreement. This book describes the privileges and immunities generally owed by the U.S. to foreign diplomatic, consular and international organization personnel under treaties and statutes, as well as the corresponding abuses that have been uncovered.

Chapter 1- To conduct foreign relations and promote the interests of their nationals located abroad, diplomatic and consular officers must be free to represent their respective States (i.e., countries) without hindrance by their hosts. Recognizing this, States receiving foreign diplomats and consular officers have long accorded such persons with certain privileges and immunities on the basis of comity, reciprocity, and international agreement. As international organizations have become increasingly important for multilateral relations and cooperation, representatives to and employees of such organizations have occasionally been granted privileges and immunities similar to those traditionally accorded to diplomats or consular officials.

Chapter 2- In 2007, the Department of State (State) reported that some foreign diplomats may be abusing the household workers they brought to the United States on A-3 or G-5 visas. GAO was asked to (1) determine the number of A-3 or G-5 visa holders who have alleged abuse by foreign diplomats with immunity since 2000, (2) review the U.S. government's process for investigating these allegations, and (3) assess how State ensures that its policies for issuing A-3 and G-5 visas are implemented correctly and consistently. GAO analyzed documents, interviewed officials, and conducted fieldwork at four consular posts that issue large numbers of A-3 or G-5 visas.

In: Diplomatic Immunity: Privileges and Abuses ISBN: 978-1-61324-706-8
Editor: Jonathan G. Carter

Chapter 1

IMMUNITIES ACCORDED TO FOREIGN DIPLOMATS, CONSULAR OFFICERS, AND EMPLOYEES OF INTERNATIONAL ORGANIZATIONS UNDER U.S. LAW*

Michael John Garcia

SUMMARY

To conduct foreign relations and promote the interests of their nationals located abroad, diplomatic and consular officers must be free to represent their respective States (i.e., countries) without hindrance by their hosts. Recognizing this, States receiving foreign diplomats and consular officers have long accorded such persons with certain privileges and immunities on the basis of comity, reciprocity, and international agreement. As international organizations have become increasingly important for multilateral relations and cooperation, representatives to and employees of such organizations have occasionally been granted privileges and immunities similar to those traditionally accorded to diplomats or consular officials.

This report describes the privileges and immunities generally owed by the U.S. to foreign diplomatic, consular, and international organization

---

* This is an edited, reformatted and augmented version of a Congressional Research Services publication, CRS Report for Congress Order Code RL33147, dated dated January 28, 2008.

personnel under treaties and statutes. It does not discuss certain exceptions to these immunities that may apply to U.S. citizens and legal permanent residents who are employed by international organizations or foreign embassies or consulates. Among the pertinent legal authorities are the Vienna Convention on Consular Relations, the Vienna Convention on Diplomatic Relations, the International Organizations Immunities Act, the Convention on the Privileges and Immunities of the United Nations, and the Agreement Regarding the Headquarters of the United Nations. Included are charts that detail the specific types of jurisdiction and obligations from which various categories of diplomatic and consular personnel are immune under each of these authorities.

INTRODUCTION

In order to conduct foreign relations and promote the interests of their nationals located abroad, States (i.e., countries) require secure means of communicating with their diplomats (i.e., representatives of a government who conduct relations with another government on its behalf) and consular officers (i.e., representatives of a government who promote the government's commercial interests and provide assistance to its citizens located in another country) stationed in other States. To ensure that such channels of communication are preserved, States receiving foreign diplomats and consular officers have long accorded such persons with certain privileges and immunities on the basis of comity, reciprocity, and international agreement.[1]

As political and economic contacts between States have grown, customary practices regarding diplomatic and consular immunities have increasingly been codified via bilateral or multilateral agreement. These agreements not only describe the specific privileges and immunities to be accorded to foreign diplomats and consular officers by a receiving State, but also specify those privileges and immunities owed to other members of diplomatic and consular missions, as well as towards the family members of mission members.

In recent decades, international organizations have been viewed as a means by which States may conduct multilateral relations and cooperate on issues which are transnational in scope. In order to ensure the autonomy of such organizations and prevent any member State from unreasonably interfering with organizational functions, many international organizations and their employees have been accorded certain privileges and immunities by their member States. These privileges and immunities are typically similar in scope to those accorded to foreign diplomatic missions.

This report describes the privileges and immunities generally owed to foreign diplomatic, consular, and international organization personnel under U.S. law. It does not discuss certain exceptions to these immunities that may apply to U.S. citizens and legal permanent residents who are employed by international organizations or foreign embassies or consulates. The treaties and statutes discussed in this report are:

- the Vienna Convention on Diplomatic Relations (Diplomatic Convention);[2]
- the Vienna Convention on Consular Relations (Consular Convention);[3]
- the Agreement Regarding the Headquarters of the United Nations (Headquarters Agreement);[4]
- the Convention on the Privileges and Immunities of the United Nations (U.N. Convention);[5] and
- the International Organizations Immunities Act.[6]

This report contains charts detailing the privileges and immunities provided by the legal authorities mentioned above, along with the personnel to whom such privileges and immunities apply.

It is important to note that the above-mentioned authorities are not exhaustive, and the scope of immunity due in any particular case may be governed in whole or in part by other instruments. For example, the United States is a party to many bilateral consular conventions that contain immunities provisions. In most instances, the other signatory is, along with the United States, a party to the Consular Convention. In these cases, the instrument affording greater protection to each State's consular officers is controlling.[7] Some countries with which the United States has a consular treaty are *not* parties to the Consular Convention. The immunities accorded to consular personnel of such States are governed by the appropriate bilateral treaties, not by the authority discussed in this report. Furthermore, not all international organizations are covered by the International Organizations Immunities Act (IOIA), or, as is the case with the United Nations, are covered not only by the IOIA but also by a number of international agreements.

Even where immunities are governed generally by the authorities cited in the relevant chart, individuals serving in similar positions for different countries may nevertheless enjoy different immunities. For example, the Diplomatic Relations Act, which effectively adopted the standards of the Diplomatic Convention for domestic application, provides that the President may, on the basis of reciprocal treatment, specify immunities for individual countries that are more or less favorable than those under the Convention.[8] Both the Diplomatic Convention and the Consular Convention allow the United States to apply immunities restrictively where a particular country has applied immunity rules restrictively towards American representatives.[9] Similarly, the IOIA conditions certain immunities on the basis of treatment of American representatives abroad.[10]

It must be emphasized that the immunities provided to foreign diplomats, consular officials, and employees of international organizations may be waived by the sending State or the appropriate international organization, with or without the consent of the individual involved.[11] On the other hand, certain individual acts may lead to a waiver of immunity. For example, the initiation of civil proceedings by an otherwise exempt individual may preclude him from invoking immunity with regards to a directly-connected counterclaim.[12] Another example of this type of personal waiver is the relinquishment of all immunity by consular employees and staff who undertake private gainful employment in the receiving State.[13] Still another example is when a foreign person accorded immunity wishes to become a lawful permanent resident of the United States, in which case the person must waive the rights, privileges, immunities, and exemptions he would otherwise accrue on account of his occupational status.[14]

Finally, note that even where an individual enjoys immunity from jurisdiction, a person harmed by the immune individual nevertheless may have recourse to compensation under one of two statutes. First, the Diplomatic Relations Act requires that (1) each diplomatic mission in the United States (including otherwise immune missions to international organizations), (2) members of these missions and their families, and (3) high ranking United Nations officials all meet liability insurance requirements relating to the operation of motor vehicles in the United States.[15] Second, the Foreign Sovereign Immunities Act provides that a foreign State shall not, with limited exception, be immune from suit for money damages being sought against it for harm occurring in the United States and caused by a wrongful nondiscretionary act of one of its officials or employees acting within the scope of duty.[16]

OVERVIEW OF APPLICABLE STATUTES AND TREATIES

The following sections provide an overview of the statutes and agreements governing the privileges and immunities accorded to foreign diplomats, consular officials, employees of international organizations, and related personnel.

Vienna Convention on Diplomatic Relations

Pursuant to its treaty obligations under the Vienna Convention on Diplomatic Relations (VCDR), ratified in 1972, the United States accords certain privileges and immunities to designated categories of persons employed by other Convention parties' diplomatic missions, along with the household family members of certain mission employees. Persons entitled to certain privileges and immunities under the Diplomatic Convention include diplomatic agents and their immediate household families, the mission's administrative and technical staff and the immediate household families of those staff members; the mission's service staff; and private servants of members of the mission.

Under the Convention, the United States accords diplomatic agents (and members of their households) absolute immunity from its criminal jurisdiction and near-absolute immunity from U.S. civil and administrative jurisdiction. A diplomatic agent is also not obliged to give evidence as a witness.[17] Below the rank of diplomat, the administrative, technical, and service staffs also are immune from criminal jurisdiction, but have more limited immunity from civil and administrative jurisdiction.[18] The household family members of diplomatic agents and mission staff are also generally provided with the same privileges and immunities accorded to the diplomatic agent or mission staff member to which they are related.[19] To varying degrees, persons covered by the Diplomatic Convention also receive immunity from taxes and customs duties, military and public service obligations, and alien registration requirements.

Congress passed the Diplomatic Relations Act to grant the privileges and immunities accorded under the Diplomatic Convention to all foreign diplomatic missions, personnel, and the families of such personnel, regardless of whether the sending State is a party to the Convention.[20] This extension is subject to the sending State's reciprocal treatment towards U.S. diplomatic missions, personnel, and families of such personnel, along with other terms and conditions the President deems appropriate.[21]

Vienna Convention on Consular Relations

The Vienna Convention on Consular Relations (VCCR), which was ratified by the U.S. in 1969, accords certain privileges and immunities to consular officers (i.e., persons who exercise consular functions on behalf of the sending State, notably including the consular post) and their immediate household families; the post's administrative and technical staff and the immediate household families of those staff members; the post's service staff; and honorary consuls (i.e., consular officers other than career consular officers). These privileges and immunities are lesser in scope than those enjoyed by similarly-situated members of diplomatic missions and those members' household families. For example, while foreign diplomats and their family members receive full immunity from the criminal jurisdiction of the receiving State under the Diplomatic Convention, consular officers covered by the Consular Convention only receive immunity for actions they take in the course of their official functions,[22] and their family members receive no immunity from the criminal jurisdiction of the receiving State. Family members of consular employees also receive no immunity from the receiving State's civil jurisdiction. Members of the consular post and their family members do receive varying degrees of immunity from the receiving State's taxes and custom duties,[23] alien registration requirements,[24] and military service obligations.[25]

The privileges and immunities owed under the Consular Convention only apply between Convention parties. The privileges and immunities owed by the U.S. to the consular personnel of non-Convention parties are governed by applicable bilateral treaty. In the case that the U.S. and another Convention party also have a bilateral treaty governing consular relations, the instrument providing broader coverage is controlling.[26]

International Organizations Immunities Act

The IOIA provides a significant number of privileges and immunities for international organizations designated by the President via executive order. Certain privileges and immunities are also accorded to employees, officials, and representatives to such organizations, along with members of their immediate families, though these are less than those accorded to the international organizations themselves. Officials, employees, and representatives to designated international organizations are accorded immunity pursuant to the IOIA following validated notification to the Secretary of State of their organizational position. The terms "official," "employee," and "representative" are not defined by the IOIA The United Nations was designated as an "international organization" for purposes of the IOIA immediately following the statute's enactment.[27] Several dozen other international organizations have been designated as receiving coverage under the IOIA, including such organizations as the International Monetary Fund,[28] the International Committee of the Red Cross,[29] the Organization of American States,[30] the World Health Organization,[31] and the World Trade Organization.[32]

U.N. Convention on Privileges and Immunities

In the same year the IOIA was enacted, the U.N. General Assembly also adopted the Convention on the Privileges and Immunities of the United Nations, establishing *de minimus* standards for the immunities and privileges accorded to the United Nations and U.N. officials, Member State representatives, and experts working for U.N. missions. These immunities and privileges are largely similar to those accorded via the IOIA.[33] The United States ratified the Convention in 1970.

As with the IOIA, the U.N. Convention on Privileges and Immunities (UNCPI) does not define the term "employee" or "official," though this is perhaps of little concern because the U.N. Convention provides immunity only to those categories of U.N. officials (beyond the U.N. Secretary-General and all Assistant Secretary-Generals) *designated* by the Secretary-General to receive protection under the Convention.[34] The Convention also does not define "experts on missions" who receive immunity under the U.N. Convention. However, an advisory decision by the International Court of Justice (which has ultimate authority to interpret the U.N. Convention),[35] found that the category of experts on U.N. missions includes, *inter alia*, persons entrusted by the United Nations with mediating disputes, preparing reports and studies, conducting investigations, or finding and establishing facts on behalf of U.N. missions.[36] The Convention defines "representatives" of U.N. Member States as including all delegates, advisors, and secretaries of Member State delegations.[37]

Besides granting an explicit set of privileges and immunities to designated persons, the U.N. Convention also specifies that certain designated individuals (i.e., U.N. representatives, the U.N. Secretary-General, all Assistant Secretary-Generals, and certain U.N. officials *designated* to receive protection under the Convention by the Secretary-General) are to receive most or all of the privileges and immunities accorded by a receiving State to diplomatic envoys. Accordingly, by reference to other statutes and treaties adopted by the receiving State, the U.N. Convention provides these U.N. officials and representatives with certain privileges and immunities beyond those explicitly described under the U.N. Convention. Generally speaking, the U.N. officials and representatives covered by the U.N. Convention are given the same privileges and immunities as those the U.S. accords to diplomats under the Diplomatic Convention. With respect to designated U.N. officials, however, Diplomatic Convention standards concerning immunity from criminal prosecution apparently are not so incorporated, as the U.N. Convention provides that such officials are immune only for official acts.[38]

U.N. Headquarters Agreement

In 1947, the United States entered the Headquarters Agreement with the United Nations. The U.N. Headquarters Agreement (UNHQA) primarily concerns the privileges and immunities accorded to the United Nations and its headquarters in New York. However, the Agreement also provides certain privileges and immunities for specified U.N. representatives and related personnel *residing in the United States*.

The Headquarters Agreement provides such persons with the full protections accorded to diplomatic envoys — a broader scope of immunity than that provided under either the IOIA or the U.N. Convention.[39] Representatives and related personnel of U.N. Member States whose governments are not recognized by the United States receive lesser privileges and immunities.[40]

Charts of Privileges and Immunities Accorded to Persons Working for Foreign Embassies, Consulates, International Organizations

The following charts list the major privileges and immunities accorded to persons working for foreign embassies, consulates, or international organizations (including, specifically, the United Nations). When a treaty or international agreement makes reference to covered personnel receiving the same immunities accorded to persons covered by other treaties, the nature of such immunities is explained. Thus, for example, because the U.N. Convention on Privileges and Immunities provides that certain U.N. personnel are to receive the same immunities as the receiving State accords diplomatic envoys, the chart detailing the immunities provided under the U.N. Convention occasionally makes references to immunities provided to diplomats under the Vienna Convention on Diplomatic Relations.

It is important to note that the charts concerning the Vienna Convention on Diplomatic Relations and the Vienna Convention on Consular Relations only discuss those immunities accorded to persons who are not U.S. nationals or permanent residents. Diplomatic and consular officers working on behalf of a foreign State who are U.S. nationals or permanent residents only receive immunity for official acts performed in the exercise of their functions, while other diplomatic or consular personnel or members of their household families receive no immunities if they are U.S. nationals or permanent residents. Persons who are employed by international organizations or are foreign representatives to such organizations are provided with immunity regardless of whether they are U.S. nationals or permanent residents.

Chart 1. Privileges and Immunities Accorded to Persons under the VCDR

Provision	Diplomatic Agents	Household Family Members of a Diplomatic Agent	Administrative & Technical Staff	Household Family Members of Administrative and Technical Staff	Service Staff	Private Servants of Members of the Mission
Definition	Head of a mission or a member of the mission staff having diplomatic rank. VCDR, art. 1(d), (e).	Not defined by the VCDR.	Staff members employed in the administrative and technical service of the mission. VCDR, art. 1(f).	Not defined by the VCDR.	Staff members in the domestic service of the mis-sion. VCDR, art. 1(g).	Persons who are in the domestic service of a member of the mission and who are not employees of the sending State. VCDR, art. 1(h).
Criminal Jurisdiction	Immune from jurisdic-tion. VCDR, art. 31(1).	Same as diplomatic agents. VCDR, art. 37(1).	Immune only for acts performed in the course of official duties. VCDR, art. 37(2).	Same as administrative and technical staff. VCDR, art. 37(2).	Immune with re-spect to acts performed in the course of duties. VCDR, art. 37(3).	No immunity under the VCDR. Jurisdic-tion to be asserted so as not to interfere unduly with the functions of the mission. VCDR, art. 37(4).

Provision	Diplomatic Agents	Household Family Members of a Diplomatic Agent	Administrative & Technical Staff	Household Family Members of Administrative and Technical Staff	Service Staff	Private Servants of Members of the Mission
Civil Jurisdiction	Immune except for (a) certain actions relating to real property, (b) estate matters in which the agent is acting as private party, and (c) actions relating to private professional or commercial activities. VCDR, art. 31(1). Must have vehicle insurance under 22 U.S.C. § 254e.	Same as diplomatic agents. VCDR, art. 37(1); 22 U.S.C. § 254e.	Immune with respect to acts performed in the course of official duties. VCDR, art. 37(2). Must have vehicle insurance under 22 U.S.C. § 254e.	Same as administrative and technical staff. VCDR, art. 37(2); 22 U.S.C. § 254e.	Same as administrative and technical staff. VCDR, art. 37(3); 22 U.S.C. § 254e.	No immunity under the Convention. Jurisdiction to be asserted so as not to interfere unduly with the functions of the mission. VCDR, art. 37(4).
Judicial Process	Immune from obligation to give evidence. Immune from execution of judgments except in non-immune civil action where execution will not infringe on the inviolability of his person or residence.	Same as diplomatic agents. VCDR, art. 37(1).	Generally immune to same degree as diplomatic agents, except immune from the execution in a civil judgment only if it concerns acts	Same as administrative and technical staff. VCDR, art. 37(2).	Immune with respect to acts performed in the course of duties. VCDR, art. 37(3).	No immunity under the VCDR. Jurisdiction to be asserted so as not to interfere unduly with the functions of the mission. VCDR, art. 37(4).

Chart 1. (Continued).

Provision	Diplomatic Agents	Household Family Members of a Diplomatic Agent	Administrative & Technical Staff	Household Family Members of Administrative and Technical Staff	Service Staff	Private Servants of Members of the Mission
	VCDR, art. 31(2), (3). Private residence deemed inviolable to same degree as diplomatic mission. VCDR, art. 30.		performed in the course of official duties. VCDR, art. 37(2).			
Taxes	Immune other than for (a) indirect taxes in the price of goods/services; (b) real property taxes/fees on private immovable property, unless held on behalf of sending State; (c) estate/ inheritance taxes on property which was not brought from sending State; (d) income tax on private income;	Same as diplomatic agents. VCDR, art. 37(1).	Same as diplomatic agents. VCDR, art. 37(2).	Same as diplomatic agents. VCDR, art. 37(2).	Exempt from dues and taxes on emoluments received by reason of their employment. VCDR, art. 37(3).	Same as service staff. VCDR, art. 37(4).

Provision	Diplomatic Agents	Household Family Members of a Diplomatic Agent	Administrative & Technical Staff	Household Family Members of Administrative and Technical Staff	Service Staff	Private Servants of Members of the Mission
	(e) charges for services rendered; and (f) court, registration, or record fees, mortgage dues and stamp duty, with respect to non-mission, immovable property. VCDR, art. 34.					
Customs	Immune from duties on articles for personal or official use. Exempt from inspection except where there are serious grounds to believe there are contraband articles or articles not for personal or official use. VCDR, art. 36.	Same as diplomatic agents. VCDR, art. 37(1).	Immune only from duties on articles imported at time of first installation. VCDR, art. 37(2).	Same as administrative and technical staff. VCDR, art. 37(2).	None, except to the extent that customs may relate to acts performed in the course of the duty. VCDR, art. 37(3).	No immunity under the Convention. Jurisdiction to be asserted so as not to interfere unduly with the functions of the mission. VCDR, art. 37(4).

Chart 1. (Continued).

Provision	Diplomatic Agents	Household Family Members of a Diplomatic Agent	Administrative & Technical Staff	Household Family Members of Administrative and Technical Staff	Service Staff	Private Servants of Members of the Mission
Social Security	Exempt with respect to services rendered for the sending State. Not exempt with respect to personal servants who are U.S. nationals or permanent residents, or who are not covered by social security provisions of the sending State or a third State. VCDR, art. 33(1)-(2).	Same as diplomatic agents. VCDR, art. 37(1).	Same as diplomatic agents. VCDR, art. 37(2).	Same as diplomatic agents. VCDR, art. 37(2).	Same as diplomatic agents. VCDR, art. 37(3).	No immunity under the Convention. Jurisdiction to be asserted so as not to interfere unduly with the functions of the mission. VCDR, art. 37(4).
Military Service, Public Service	Immune from all public service and military obligations. VCDR, art. 35.	Same as diplomatic agents. VCDR, art. 37(1).	Same as diplomatic agents. VCDR, art. 37(2).	Same as diplomatic agents. VCDR, art. 37(2).	No immunity in Convention, but may be exempt under 50 App. U.S.C. App. § 456.	No immunity under the Convention. Jurisdiction to be asserted so as not to interfere unduly with the functions of the mission. VCDR, art. 37(4).

Provision	Diplomatic Agents	Household Family Members of a Diplomatic Agent	Administrative & Technical Staff	Household Family Members of Administrative and Technical Staff	Service Staff	Private Servants of Members of the Mission
Immigration	No specific immunity under the Convention, but immune generally from civil and administrative jurisdiction under VCDR, art. 31.	Same as diplomatic agents. VCDR, art. 37(1).	Same as diplomatic agents, with respect to actions taken in course of official duties. VCDR, art. 37(2).	Same as administrative and technical staff. VCDR, art. 37(2).	Same as adminis-trative and techni-cal staff. VCDR, art. 37(3.)	No immunity under the Convention. Ju-risdiction to be as-serted so as not to interfere unduly with the functions of the mission. VCDR, art. 37(4).

Chart 2. Privileges and Immunities Accorded to Persons Under the VCCR

Provision	Consular Officer	Household Family Members of Consular Officer	Consular Employee	Household Family Members of Consular Employees	Service Staff	Honorary Consul
Definition	Any person, including the head of a consular post, entrusted in that capacity with the exercise of consular functions. VCCR, art. 1(d).	Not defined by the VCCR.	Any person employed in the administrative or technical service of a consular post. VCCR, art. 1(e).	Not defined by the VCCR.	Any person employed in the domestic service of a consular post. VCCR, art. 1(f).	Consular officer other than career consular officer of the sending State. VCCR, art 1(2).

Chart 2. (Continued).

Provision	Consular Officer	Household Family Members of Consular Officer	Consular Employee	Household Family Members of Consular Employees	Service Staff	Honorary Consul
Criminal Jurisdiction	Immune from jurisdiction with respect to acts performed in the exercise of consular functions. Immune from arrest and detention pending trial, except in case of grave crime pursuant to a decision by a judicial authority. Criminal proceedings to be conducted so as not to interfere unduly with consular functions. VCCR, arts. 41, 43.	No immunity under the VCCR.	Immune from jurisdiction in respect to acts performed in the exercise of consular functions. VCCR, art. 43.	No immunity under the VCCR.	No immunity under the VCCR.	No immunity from arrest, detention, or prosecution, but proceedings are to be carried out expeditiously with as little interference with official functions as circumstances will allow. VCCR, art. 63.

Provision	Consular Officer	Household Family Members of Consular Officer	Consular Employee	Household Family Members of Consular Employees	Service Staff	Honorary Consul
Civil Jurisdiction	Immune from civil and administrative jurisdiction with respect to acts performed in exercise of functions except (1) to degree that an action relates to private contract other than on behalf of sending State or (2) actions by 3rd parties for vehicle-caused damage. VCCR, art. 43.	No immunity under the VCCR.	Same as consular officers. VCCR, art. 43.	No immunity under the VCCR.	No immunity under the VCCR.	Same as consular officers. VCCR, art. 58(2).
Judicial Process	Immune from contempt for failure to give evidence whenever called upon to do so. Evidence, when provided, may be given so as not to interfere with consular functions. VCCR, art. 44.	No immunity under the VCCR.	Immune only with respect to giving evidence concerning official functions or documents, or concerning expert testimony on sending State's law. VCCR, art. 44.	No immunity under the VCCR.	As members of consular post, have same degree of immunity as consular employees. VCCR, arts. 1(g), 44.	Same as consular employees. VCCR, art 58(2).

Chart 2. (Continued).

Provision	Consular Officer	Household Family Members of Consular Officer	Consular Employee	Household Family Members of Consular Employees	Service Staff	Honorary Consul
Taxes	Immune from taxes other than (a) indirect taxes in the price of goods/services; (b) real property taxes/fees on private immovable property, unless held for sending State; (c) inheritance and estate taxes on property not brought from sending State; (d) income tax on private U.S. income; (e) charges on specific services; and (f) court, registration, or record fees, mortgage dues and stamp duties on non-mission property. VCDR, art. 34.	Same as consular officers. VCCR, art. 49(1).	Same as consular officers. VCCR, art. 49(1).	Same as consular officers. VCCR, art. 49(1).	Exempt from dues and taxes on wages received for their services. VCCR, art 49(2).	Exempt from all dues and taxes on remuneration and emoluments received for performing consular functions. VCCR, art. 66.

Provision	Consular Officer	Household Family Members of Consular Officer	Consular Employee	Household Family Members of Consular Employees	Service Staff	Honorary Consul
Customs	Immune from duties on articles for personal or official use. Exempt from inspection except where there are serious grounds to believe there are contraband articles or articles not for personal or official use. VCCR, art. 50(1).	Same as consular officers. VCCR, art. 50(1).	Generally the same as consular officers with respect to articles imported at the time of fist installation. VCCR, art. 50(2). However, no immunity concerning personal inspection of baggage.	No immunity under VCCR.	No immunity under VCCR.	Immune only with respect to customs duties on certain consular office items. VCCR, art. 62.
Social Security	Exempt with respect to services rendered for the sending State. Not exempt with respect to personal servants who are U.S. nationals or permanent residents, or are not covered by social security provisions of the sending State or a third State. VCCR, art. 48(1).	Same as consular officers. VCCR, art. 48(1).	Same as consular officers. VCCR, art. 48(1).	Same as consular officers. VCCR, art. 48(1).	Same as consular officers. VCCR, art. 48(1).	No immunity provision separate from that concerning taxes and dues on all emoluments and remuneration in respect to official functions. VCCR, art. 66.

Chart 2. (Continued).

Provision	Consular Officer	Household Family Members of Consular Officer	Consular Employee	Household Family Members of Consular Employees	Service Staff	Honorary Consul
Military Service, Public Service Immigration	Immune from all public service and military obligations. VCCR, art. 52. Exempt from all laws regarding registration of aliens and residency permits. VCCR, art. 46.	Same as consular officers. VCCR, art. 52. Same as consular officials. VCCR, art. 46.	Same as consular officers. VCCR, art. 52. Exempt from registration and residency permit requirements if permanent employee of sending State and are not engaged in private gainful occupation in the United States. VCCR, art. 46.	Same as consular officers. VCCR, art. 52. Exempt only to same degree as principal consular employee. VCCR, art. 46.	Same as consular officers. VCCR, art. 52. No immunity under the VCCR.	Same as consular officers. VCCR, art. 67. Exempt from registration and residency permit requirements, unless also engaged in private gainful occupation in the U.S. VCCR, art. 65.

Chart 3. Privileges and Immunities Accorded to Persons Under the UNCPI and UNHQA

Provision	Resident Representatives of Member States	Representatives of Member States (generally)	Secretary General, Assistant Secretaries General, Their Spouses and Minor Children	Designated U.N. Officials	Experts on U.N. Missions
Definition	All delegates, deputy delegates, advisors, technical experts and designated by Member State with agreement, where relevant, of the U.N. or United States. UNHQA, § 15.	All delegates, deputy delegates, advisers, technical experts and secretaries of delegations. UNCPI, § 16.	Not expressly defined.	Individuals within categories of officials designated by the Secretary-General as entitled to immunities. UNCPI, §17.	Not expressly defined.
Criminal Jurisdiction	Same as diplomatic envoys. UNCPI, § 11(g); UNHQA, § 15. In U.S., full immunity from criminal jurisdiction. VCDR, art. 31(1).	Same as resident representatives (i.e., receive same immunities accorded to diplomatic envoys). UNCPI, § 11(g); VCDR, art. 31(1).	Same as representatives of U.N. Member States (i.e., receive same immunities accorded to diplomatic envoys). UNCPI, § 19; VCDR, art. 31(1).	Immune with respect to official acts. UNCPI, § 18(a).	Immune from personal arrest and detention. Immune with respect to official acts. UNCPI, § 22(a), (b).
Civil Jurisdiction	Same as diplomatic envoys. UNCPI, § 11(g); UNHQA, § 15. Immune except for (a) certain actions relating to real property, (b) estate matters in which the agent is acting as private party, and (c) actions relating to private professional or commercial activities. VCDR, art. 31(1).	Same as resident representatives (i.e., receive same immunities accorded to diplomatic envoys). UNCPI, § 11(g); VCDR, art. 31(1).	Same as resident representatives (i.e., receive same immunities accorded to diplomatic envoys). Must have vehicle insurance. UNCPI, § 19; 22 U.S.C. § 254e.	Immune with respect to official acts. UNCPI, § 18(a).	Immune with respect to official acts. UNCPI, § 22(b).

Chart 3. (Continued).

Provision	Resident Representatives of Member States	Representatives of Member States (generally)	Secretary General, Assistant Secretaries General, Their Spouses and Minor Children	Designated U.N. Officials	Experts on U.N. Missions
Judicial Process	Same as diplomatic envoys. UNCPI, § 11(g); UNHQA, § 15. In U.S., immune from obligation to give evidence. Immune from execution of judgments except in non-immune civil action where execution will not infringe on the inviolability of his person or residence. VCDR, art. 31(2)-(3). Private residence deemed inviolable to same degree as diplomatic mission. VCDR, art. 30.	Same as resident representatives (i.e., receive same immunities accorded to diplomatic envoys). UNCPI, § 11(g); VCDR arts. 30, 31(2)-(3).	Same as resident representatives (i.e., receive same immunities accorded to diplomatic envoys). UNCPI, § 19; VCDR arts. 30, 31(2)-(3).	Immune with respect to official acts. UNCPI, § 18(a).	Immune with respect to official acts. UNCPI, § 22(b).

Provision	Resident Representatives of Member States	Representatives of Member States (generally)	Secretary General, Assistant Secretaries General, Their Spouses and Minor Children	Designated U.N. Officials	Experts on U.N. Missions
Taxes	Same as diplomatic envoys. UNCPI, § 11(g); UNHQA, § 15. In U.S., immune from taxes other than (a) indirect taxes in the price of goods or services; (b) real property taxes and fees on private immovable property, unless held on behalf of sending State; (c) estate and inheritance taxes not attributable to property brought from sending State; (d) income tax on private income earned in U.S.; (e) charges levied for specific services rendered; and (f) registration, court or record fees, mortgage dues and stamp duty, with respect to immovable property, other than mission premises. VCDR, art. 34.	Same as resident representatives (i.e., receive same immunities accorded to diplomatic envoys), except with respect to excise duties and sales taxes. UNCPI, § 11(g); VCDR, art. 34.	Same as resident representatives (i.e., receive same immunities accorded to diplomatic envoys). UNCPI, § 19; VCDR, art. 34.	Immune from taxes on salaries and emoluments paid by the U.N. UNCPI, § 18(b).	No express immunity, beyond general immunity necessary for the independent exercise of their functions. UNCPI, § 22.

Chart 3. (Continued).

Provision	Resident Representatives of Member States	Representatives of Member States (generally)	Secretary General, Assistant Secretaries General, Their Spouses and Minor Children	Designated U.N. Officials	Experts on U.N. Missions
Customs	Same as diplomatic envoys. UNCPI, § 11(g); UNHQA, § 15. Immune from duties on articles for personal or official use. In U.S., exempt from inspection except where there are serious grounds to believe there are contraband articles or articles not for personal or official use. VCDR, art. 36.	Same as resident representatives (i.e., receive same immunities accorded to diplomatic envoys), except with respect to duties on goods imported other than personal baggage. UNCPI, § 11(g); VCDR, art. 36.	Same as resident representatives (i.e., receive same immunities accorded to diplomatic envoys). UNCPI, § 19; VCDR, art. 36.	Immune from duties on furniture and effects imported at the time of first taking post. UNCPI, § 18(g).	Same immunities as diplomatic envoys as to personal baggage. UNCPI, § 22(f). In U.S., exempt from inspection except where there are serious grounds to believe there are contraband articles or articles not for personal or official use. VCDR, art. 36.

Provision	Resident Representatives of Member States	Representatives of Member States (generally)	Secretary General, Assistant Secretaries General, Their Spouses and Minor Children	Designated U.N. Officials	Experts on U.N. Missions
Social Security	Same as diplomatic envoys. UNCPI, § 11(g); UNHQA, § 15. In U.S., exempt with respect to services rendered for the sending State. Not exempt with respect to personal servants who are U.S. nationals or permanent residents, or are not covered by social security provisions of the sending State or a third State. VCDR, art. 33(1)-(2).	Same as resident representatives (i.e., receive same immunities accorded to diplomatic envoys). UNCPI, § 11(g); VCDR, art. 33(1)-(2).	Same as resident representatives (i.e., receive same immunities accorded to diplomatic envoys). UNCPI, § 11(g); VCDR, art. 33(1)-(2).	No express immunity other than for taxes on U.N. salaries and emoluments. UNCPI, § 18.	No express immunity, beyond general immunity necessary for the independent exercise of their functions. UNCPI, § 22.
Military Service, Public Service	Exempt, along with spouses, from national service obligations. UNCPI, § 11(d). Generally immune on same basis as diplomatic envoys. UNHQA, §. 15; UNCPI, § 11(g). In U.S., immune from all public service and military obligations. VCDR, art. 35.	Exempt, along with spouses, from national service obligations to same degree as resident representatives. UNCPI, § 11(d), (g); VCDR, art. 35.	Exempt, along with spouses, from national service obligations to same degree as resident representatives. UNCPI, § 19; VCDR, art. 35.	Exempt from national service obligations. UNCPI, § 18(c).	No express immunity, beyond general immunity necessary for the independent exercise of their functions. UNCPI, § 22.

Chart 3. (Continued).

Provision	Resident Representatives of Member States	Representatives of Member States (generally)	Secretary General, Assistant Secretaries General, Their Spouses and Minor Children	Designated U.N. Officials	Experts on U.N. Missions
Immigration	Exempt, along with spouses, from immigration restriction and alien registration requirements. UNCPI, § 11(d). Generally immune on same basis as diplomatic envoys. UNHQA, § 15; UNCPI, § 11(g).	Along with spouses, same as resident representatives. UNCPI,§ 11(d), (g).	Exempt, along with spouses and dependent relatives, from immigration restrictions and alien restrictions. UNCPI, §§ 18(d), 19.	Along with spouses and dependent relatives, same as Secretary General. UNCPI,§ 18(d).	No express immunity, beyond general immunity necessary for the independent exercise of their functions. UNCPI, § 22.

Chart 4. Privileges and Immunities Accorded to Persons Under the IOIA and Other Relevant Domestic Statutes

Provision	Foreign Representatives to, and Officials and Employees of, International Organizations
Definition	Not specifically defined by statute.
Criminal Jurisdiction	Immune with respect to official acts falling within their functions. IOIA, § 288d(b).
Civil Jurisdiction	Immune with respect to official acts falling within their functions. IOIA, § 288d(b).
Judicial Process	Immune with respect to official acts falling within their functions. IOIA, § 288d(b).
Taxes	Exempt from tax on compensation for official services except where employed by a foreign government that does not grant an equivalent exemption to U.S. government employees. 26 U.S.C. § 893.

Provision	Foreign Representatives to, and Officials and Employees of, International Organizations
Customs	Immune, along with immediate household family members, from duties with respect to baggage and effects imported in connection with the arrival of the owner. IOIA, § 288(b).
Social Security	Exempt from Social Security contributions related to employment in or representation to the international organization. 26 U.S.C. § 3121(b)(15).
Military Service, Public Service	No immunity under IOIA. Exemption from military service apparently depends on previous service abroad, applicable treaties, and immigration status. 50 App. U.S.C. § 456(a)(1).
Immigration	Exempt, along with immediate household family members, from immigration and alien registration requirements on same basis as officers and employees, respectively, of foreign governments and their families. IOIA, § 288d(a).

Chart 5. Privileges and Immunities Accorded to U.N. Representatives and Employees Under the IOIA, UNCPI, UNHQA, VCDR, and Related Statutes and Agreements

Provision	Resident Representatives of Member States	Representatives of Member States (generally)	Secretary General, Assistant Secretaries General, Their Spouses and Minor Children	Designated U.N. Officials	Non-designated U.N. Officials and U.N. Employees	Experts on U.N. Missions
Definition	All delegates, deputy delegates, advisors, technical experts and designated by Member State with agree-ment, where relevant, of the U.N. or United States. UNHQA, § 15.	All delegates, deputy delegates, advisers, technical experts and secretaries of delega-tions. UNCPI, § 16.	Not expressly defined.	Individuals falling within categories of officials designated by the Secretary-General as entitled to immunities. UNCPI, §17.	Not expressly defined.	Not expressly defined.
Criminal Jurisdiction	Same as diplomatic envoys. UNCPI, § 11(g); UNHQA, § 15. In U.S., accorded full immunity from criminal jurisdiction. VCDR, art. 31(1).	Same as resident rep-resentatives (i.e., re-ceive same immuni-ties accorded to diplomatic envoys). UNCPI, § 11(g); VCDR, art. 31(1).	Same as resident representatives (i.e., receive same immuni-ties accorded to diplo-matic envoys). UNCPI, § 19; VCDR, art. 31(1).	Immune with respect to official acts. UNCPI,§ 18(a); IOIA, § 288d(b).	Same as designated U.N. officials. IOIA, § 288d(b).	Immune from personal arrest and detention. UNCPI, § 22(a). Immune with respect to official acts. UNCPI, § 22(b); IOIA, § 288d(b).

Provision	Resident Representatives of Member States	Representatives of Member States (generally)	Secretary General, Assistant Secretaries General, Their Spouses and Minor Children	Designated U.N. Officials	Non-designated U.N. Officials and U.N. Employees	Experts on U.N. Missions
Civil Jurisdiction	Same as diplomatic envoys. UNCPI, § 11(g); UNHQA, § 15. In U.S., immune except for (a) certain actions relating to real property, (b) estate matters in which the agent is acting as private party, and (c) actions relating to private professional or commercial activities. VCDR, art. 31(1).	Same as resident representatives (i.e., receive same immunities accorded to diplomatic envoys). UNCPI, § 11(g); VCDR, art. 31(1).	Same as resident representatives (i.e., receive same immunities accorded to diplomatic envoys). UNCPI, § 19; VCDR, art. 31(1). Must have vehicle insurance under 22 U.S.C. § 254e.	Immune with respect to official acts. UNCPI, § 18(a); IOIA, § 288d(b).	Same as designated U.N. officials. IOIA, § 288d(b).	Same as designated U.N. officials. UNCPI, § 22(b); IOIA, § 288d(b).

Chart 5. (Continued).

Provision	Resident Representatives of Member States	Representatives of Member States (generally)	Secretary General, Assistant Secretaries General, Their Spouses and Minor Children	Designated U.N. Officials	Non-designated U.N. Officials and U.N. Employees	Experts on U.N. Missions
Judicial Process	Receive same immunities as diplomatic envoys. UNCPI, § 11(g); UNHQA, § 15. Immune from obligation to give evidence. Immune from execution of judgments except in non-immune civil action where execution will not infringe on the inviolability of his person or residence. VCDR, art. 31(2)-(3).	Same as resident representatives (i.e., receive same immunities accorded to diplomatic envoys). UNCPI, § 11(g); VCDR, arts. 30, 31(2)-(3).	Same as resident representatives (i.e., receive same immunities accorded to diplomatic envoys). UNCPI, § 11(g); VCDR, arts. 30, 31(2)-(3).	Immune with respect to official acts. UNCPI, § 18(a); IOIA, § 288d(b).	Same as designated U.N. officials. IOIA, § 288d(b).	Same as designated U.N. officials. UNCPI, § 22(b).

Provision	Resident Representatives of Member States	Representatives of Member States (generally)	Secretary General, Assistant Secretaries General, Their Spouses and Minor Children	Designated U.N. Officials	Non-designated U.N. Officials and U.N. Employees	Experts on U.N. Missions
	Private residence deemed inviolable to same degree as diplomatic mission. VCDR, art. 30.					
Taxes	Same as diplomatic envoys. UNHQA, § 15. Immune from taxes other than (a) indirect taxes in price of goods/services; (b) real property taxes/fees on private property, unless held on behalf of sending State;	Same as resident representatives (i.e., receive same immunities as diplomatic envoys), except with respect to excise duties and sales taxes. UNCPI, § 11(g).	Same as resident representatives (i.e., receive same immunities as diplomatic envoys). UNCPI, § 19.	Immune from taxes on salaries and emoluments paid by the U.N. UNCPI, § 18(b).	Immune from taxes on salaries and emoluments paid by the U.N. 26 U.S.C. § 893.	If employed by the U.N., immune from taxes on salaries and emoluments paid by the U.N. 26 U.S.C. § 893. Have general immunity necessary for the independent exercise of functions. UNCPI, § 22.

Chart 5. (Continued).

Provision	Resident Representatives of Member States	Representatives of Member States (generally)	Secretary General, Assistant Secretaries General, Their Spouses and Minor Children	Designated U.N. Officials	Non-designated U.N. Officials and U.N. Employees	Experts on U.N. Missions
	(c) estate or inheritance taxes on property other than that brought from sending State; (d) income tax on private U.S. income; (e) charges for specific services; and (f) registration, court or record fees, mortgage dues and stamp duty, with respect to non-mission, immovable, property. VCDR, art. 34.					

Provision	Resident Representatives of Member States	Representatives of Member States (generally)	Secretary General, Assistant Secretaries General, Their Spouses and Minor Children	Designated U.N. Officials	Non-designated U.N. Officials and U.N. Employees	Experts on U.N. Missions
Customs	Same as diplomatic envoys. UNCPI, § 11(g); UNHQA, § 15. Immune from duties on articles for personal or official use. In U.S., exempt from inspection except where there are serious grounds to believe there are contraband articles or articles not for personal or official use. VCDR, art. 36.	Same as resident representatives, including with respect to immunities accorded to immediate household family members. UNCPI, § 11(g); VCDR, art. 36; IOIA, § 288(b).	Same as resident representatives, including with respect to immunities accorded to immediate household family members. UNCPI, § 11(g); VCDR, art. 36; IOIA, § 288(b).	Immune, along with immediate household family members, from duties with respect to baggage and effects imported in connection with the arrival of the owner. IOIA, § 288(b).	Same as designated U.N. officials. IOIA, § 288(b).	Same immunities as resident representatives with respect to personal baggage. UNCPI, § 22(f); VCDR, art. 36. If employed by U.N., experts and immediate household family members are immune from duties with respect to baggage and effects imported in connection with the arrival of the owner. IOIA, § 288(b).

Chart 5. (Continued).

Provision	Resident Representatives of Member States	Representatives of Member States (generally)	Secretary General, Assistant Secretaries General, Their Spouses and Minor Children	Designated U.N. Officials	Non-designated U.N. Officials and U.N. Employees	Experts on U.N. Missions
	Immediate household family members are immune from duties with respect to baggage and effects imported in connection with the arrival of the owner. IOIA, § 288(b).					
Social Security	Same as diplomatic envoys. UNCPI, § 11(g); UNHQA, § 15. Exempt with respect to services rendered for the sending State.	Same as resident representatives (i.e., receive same immunities as diplomatic envoys). UNCPI, § 11(g); VCDR, art. 33(1)-(2).	Same as resident representatives (i.e., receive same immunities as diplomatic envoys). UNCPI, § 19; VCDR, art. 33(1)-(2).	Exempt from Social Security contributions related to employment in or representation to the international organization. 26 U.S.C. § 3121(b)(15).	Same as designated U.N. officials. 26 U.S.C. § 3121(b)(15).	General immunity necessary for the independent exercise of their functions. UNCPI, § 22. If employed by U.N., same immunity as designated U.N. officials. 26 U.S.C. 3121(b)(15).

Provision	Resident Representatives of Member States	Representatives of Member States (generally)	Secretary General, Assistant Secretaries General, Their Spouses and Minor Children	Designated U.N. Officials	Non-designated U.N. Officials and U.N. Employees	Experts on U.N. Missions
	Not exempt with respect to personal servants who are U.S. nationals or permanent residents, or are not covered by social security provisions of the sending State or a third State. VCDR, art. 33(1)-(2).					
Military Service, Public Service	Exempt, along with spouses, from national service obligations. UNCPI, § 11(d). Generally immune on same basis as diplomatic envoys.	Exempt, along with spouses, to same degree as resident representatives (i.e., immune on same basis as diplomatic envoys). UNCPI, § 11(g); VCDR, art. 35.	Exempt, along with spouses, to same degree as resident representatives (i.e., immune on same basis as diplomatic envoys). UNCPI, § 19; VCDR, art. 35.	Exempt from national service obligations. UNCPI, § 18(c).	No express immunity. Exemption apparently depends on previous service abroad, applicable treaties, and immigration status. 50 App. U.S.C. § 456(a)(1).	No express immunity, beyond general immunity necessary for the independent exercise of their functions. UNCPI, § 22.

Chart 5. (Continued).

Provision	Resident Representatives of Member States	Representatives of Member States (generally)	Secretary General, Assistant Secretaries General, Their Spouses and Minor Children	Designated U.N. Officials	Non-designated U.N. Officials and U.N. Employees	Experts on U.N. Missions
	UNHQA, §. 15; UNCPI, § 11(g). In U.S., immune from all public service and military obligations. VCDR, art. 35.					Exemption apparently depends on previous service abroad, applicable treaties, and immigration status. 50 App. U.S.C. § 456(a)(1).
Immigration	Exempt, along with spouses, from immigration restriction and alien registration requirements. UNCPI, § 11(d).	Same as resident representatives (including with respect to immunities accorded to spouses and other immediate household family members). UNCPI, § 11(d); IOIA, § 288d(a).	Exempt, along with spouses and dependent relatives, from immigration restrictions and alien restrictions. UNCPI, §§ 18(d), 19.	Same as Secretary General (including with respect to immunities accorded to spouses, dependent relatives, and other immediate household family members). UNCPI, §§ 18(d), 19; IOIA, § 288d(a).	Exempt, along with immediate household family members, from immigration and alien registration requirements on same basis as officers and employees, respectively, of foreign governments and their families. IOIA, § 288d(a).	No express immunity, beyond that necessary for the independent exercise of their functions. UNCPI, § 22. If employed by U.N., exempt, along with immediate household family members to same degree as other U.N. employees. IOIA, § 288d(a).

Provision	Resident Representatives of Member States	Representatives of Member States (generally)	Secretary General, Assistant Secretaries General, Their Spouses and Minor Children	Designated U.N. Officials	Non-designated U.N. Officials and U.N. Employees	Experts on U.N. Missions
	Other immediate household family members are also exempt from immigration and alien registration requirements on same basis as officers of foreign governments and their families. IOIA, § 288d(a).		Other immediate household family members are also exempt from immigration and alien registration requirements on same basis as officers of foreign governments and their families. IOIA, § 288d(a).			

The United Nations and specified officials, employees, and representatives to the organization are accorded a number of privileges and immunities by a series of interrelated statutes and treaties. In some cases, the immunities accorded to the organization and specified officials, employees, and U.N. representatives are explicit; in other cases, they are established via cross-reference to other sources of law. This chart details the scope of such immunities, as governed by the International Organizations Immunities Act, the U.N. Convention on Privileges and Immunities, the U.N. Headquarters Agreement, and, by cross-reference, the Vienna Convention on Diplomatic Relations. Where appropriate, immunities provided by related U.S. statutes are also listed.

End Notes

[1] For background on the history of diplomatic immunity, see CRS Report RS21672, *Diplomatic Immunity: History and Overview*, by Michael John Garcia.

[2] Vienna Convention on Diplomatic Relations, April 18, 1961, 23 U.S.T. 3227, T.I.A.S. No. 7502, 500 U.N.T.S. 95 [hereinafter "Diplomatic Convention"].

[3] Vienna Convention on Consular Relations, April 24, 1963, 21 U.S.T. 77, T.I.A.S. No. 6820, 596 U.N.T.S. 261 [hereinafter "Consular Convention"].

[4] Agreement Regarding the Headquarters of the United Nations, November 21, 1947, 61 Stat. 3416, T.I.A.S. No. 1676, 11 U.N.T.S. 11. [hereinafter "Headquarters Agreement"], P.L. 80-357 (1947).

[5] Convention on the Privileges and Immunities of the United Nations, February 13, 1946, 21 U.S.T. 1418, T.I.A.S. No. 6900, 1 U.N.T.S. 15 [hereinafter "U.N. Convention"].

[6] International Organizations Immunities Act, 22 U.S.C. §§ 288 et seq. [hereinafter "IOIA"].

[7] See Consular Convention, art. 73.

[8] 22 U.S.C. § 254c.

[9] See,e.g., Diplomatic Convention, art. 47; Consular Convention, art. 72.

[10] See,e.g., IOIA § 288d.

[11] See, e.g., Diplomatic Convention, art. 32; Consular Convention, art. 45; U.N. Convention, §§ 14, 20; IOIA § 288d(b).

[12] See Diplomatic Convention, art. 32(3); see also Consular Convention, art. 45(3).

[13] See Consular Convention, art. 57(2).

[14] A foreign person with an occupational status entitling him to immunity generally enters the United States via a nonimmigrant visa. In order for the alien to adjust his status to legal permanent resident of the United States (i.e., to become an "immigrant"), the alien must submit an I-508 form, waiving the rights and privileges he would otherwise be accrued. This form may be viewed at [http://www.uscis.gov/propub/DocView/afmid/dat/I_508.pdf].

[15] 22 U.S.C. § 254e.

[16] 28 U.S.C. § 1605(a)(5).

[17] Diplomatic Convention, art. 31(2).

[18] Id. art. 37.

[19] Id. art. 37(1)-(2).

[20] 22 U.S.C. § 254c.

[21] Id.

[22] Consular Convention, arts. 41, 43.

[23] Id. arts. 49-50.

[24] Id. art. 46.

[25] Id. art. 52.

[26] Id. art. 73.

[27] Exec. Ord. No. 9698, February 19, 1946, 11 Fed. Reg. 1809.

[28] Exec. Ord. No. 9751, July 11, 1946, 11 Fed. Reg. 7713.

[29] Exec. Ord. No. 12643, June 23, 1988, 53 Fed. Reg. 24247.

[30] Exec. Ord. No. 10533, June 3, 1954, 19 Fed. Reg. 3289.

[31] Exec. Ord. No. 10025, December 30, 1948, 13 Fed. Reg. 9361.

[32] Exec. Ord. No. 13042, April 9, 1997, 50 Fed. Reg. 28301.

[33] Two notable differences are (1) the U.N. Convention provides for certain privileges and immunities for experts of U.N. missions, while the IOIA does not, and (2) the IOIA also

accords certain privileges and immunities to employees of international organizations, while the U.N. Convention does not mandate such benefits.

[34] Accordingly, non-designated officials and all other U.N. employees are not granted immunity from a local State's legal process via the U.N. Convention, though they may nevertheless receive immunity via the IOIA.

[35] U.N. Convention, §§ 29-30.

[36] See Applicability of Article VI, Section 22, of the Convention on the Privileges and Immunities of the United Nations, Advisory Opinion, 1989 ICJ Rep. 177 (December 15, 1989).

[37] U.N. Convention, § 16.

[38] Id. § 18(a).

[39] Headquarters Agreement, § 15.

[40] Id.

In: Diplomatic Immunity: Privileges and Abuses ISBN: 978-1-61324-706-8
Editor: Jonathan G. Carter

Chapter 2

HUMAN RIGHTS: U.S. GOVERNMENT'S EFFORTS TO ADDRESS ALLEGED ABUSE OF HOUSEHOLD WORKERS BY FOREIGN DIPLOMATS WITH IMMUNITY COULD BE STRENGTHENED*

United States Government Accountability Office

WHY GAO DID THIS STUDY

In 2007, the Department of State (State) reported that some foreign diplomats may be abusing the household workers they brought to the United States on A-3 or G-5 visas. GAO was asked to (1) determine the number of A-3 or G-5 visa holders who have alleged abuse by foreign diplomats with immunity since 2000, (2) review the U.S. government's process for investigating these allegations, and (3) assess how State ensures that its policies for issuing A-3 and G-5 visas are implemented correctly and consistently. GAO analyzed documents, interviewed officials, and conducted fieldwork at four consular posts that issue large numbers of A-3 or G-5 visas.

---

* This is an edited, reformatted and augmented version of the United States Government Accountability Office's publication, Report to the Subcommittee on Human Rights and the Law, Committee on the Judiciary, U.S. Senate GAO-08-892, dated July 2008.

What GAO Recommends

GAO recommends that the Secretary of State (1) collect and main records on allegations of household worker abuse by foreign diplomats, (2) establish a system alerting consular officers to seek guidance before issuing an A-3 or G-5 visa to an individual applying to work for a foreign diplomat who may have abused workers, and (3) spot-check compliance with A-3 and G-5 visa policies and procedures. GAO also recommends that the Secretaries of State and Homeland Security and the Attorney General outline a process for determining which specific techniques can be used when investigating foreign diplomats. State and the Departments of Justice and Homeland Security concurred with the recommendations addressed to them.

What GAO Found

GAO identified 42 household workers with A-3 or G-5 visas who alleged that they were abused by foreign diplomats with immunity from 2000 through 2008, but the total number is likely higher. The total number of alleged incidents since 2000 is likely higher for four reasons: household workers' fear of contacting law enforcement, nongovernmental organizations' protection of victim confidentiality, limited information on some cases handled by the U.S. government, and federal agencies' challenges identifying cases. For example, State has several offices that receive allegations of abuse by foreign diplomats, but no single office maintains information on all allegations.

The U.S. government's process for investigating alleged abuse of household workers by foreign diplomats is complicated by three factors. First, immunity can pose constraints for law enforcement in collecting evidence. Second, the status of foreign diplomats can heighten their workers' sense of vulnerability, causing the workers to fear cooperating with investigators. Third, the length of time it takes to obtain a legal opinion from State on the permissibility of using certain investigative techniques can hamper investigations. According to State, although some techniques are clearly prohibited by international law (such as searching certain diplomats' residences), the permissibility of others under international law is less clear. In advising on the use of investigative techniques, State considers legal and policy issues, such as reciprocity— assessing how U.S. diplomats abroad might be affected by actions taken toward a foreign diplomat on U.S. soil.

State may ask Justice to provide information to help determine the permissibility of certain techniques, but the process of obtaining this information can be difficult and time consuming for Justice. Although both State and Justice have discussed creating a process to avoid delays, no formal actions have, thus far, been taken to establish one.

Weaknesses exist in State's process for ensuring correct and consistent implementation of policies and procedures for issuing A-3 and G-5 visas. GAO's review of employment contracts submitted at four consular posts by A-3 and G-5 visa applicants showed that they often did not include State's required components, such as a guarantee of the minimum or prevailing wage. GAO also found that officers at the four posts were unclear about or unfamiliar with certain aspects of State's guidance. Few of the officers were aware that they should inform A-3 and G-5 visa applicants of their rights under U.S. law during their interview. Some officers at the four posts also were uncertain about the reasons for refusing A-3 or G-5 visas. State is considering adding provisions to its guidance that would more clearly stipulate reasons for refusing these visas, such as if an A-3 or G-5 applicant seeks to work for a foreign diplomat who is linked to a pattern of employee disappearance, abuse allegations, or other irregularities. However, State has not reached internal agreement on these provisions and has set no timetable for doing so. State headquarters officials said they rely on individual posts to monitor implementation of A-3 and G-5 visa policies and procedures and do not routinely assess posts' compliance.

ABBREVIATIONS

AUSA	Assistant United States Attorney
CIS	Citizenship and Immigration Services
CRT/CS	Civil Rights Division/Criminal Section
FBI	Federal Bureau of Investigation
Homeland Security	Department of Homeland Security
ICE	Immigration and Customs Enforcement
Justice	Department of Justice
Labor	Department of Labor
NGO	nongovernmental organization
State	Department of State
TOMIS	The Office of Foreign Missions Information System
USUN	U.S. Mission to the United Nations

July 29, 2008

The Honorable Richard Durbin
Chairman

The Honorable Tom Coburn, MD
Ranking Member
Subcommittee on Human Rights and the Law
Committee on Judiciary
United States Senate

In June 2007, the Department of State (State) noted in its annual Trafficking in Persons report that some foreign diplomats[1] may have abused individuals they had brought to the United States to work in their households. State again highlighted this problem in a July 2007 note to all Chiefs of Diplomatic Missions in the United States, stating that it had recently learned of a number of allegations of trafficking in persons[2] with respect to household workers, including allegations of involuntary servitude and physical abuse. A few of these cases have garnered congressional and media attention, particularly because the accused foreign diplomats held full diplomatic immunity[3] and thus could not be prosecuted in U.S. courts. For example, in 2002, a household worker accused her employers, a high-ranking diplomat and his wife, of verbally, physically, and sexually abusing her. She also alleged that they required her to work 16 to 17-hour days without any payment and prohibited her from leaving the home unaccompanied. She filed a civil lawsuit against her employers, but because they held full diplomatic immunity, the case was dismissed. The diplomat and his wife have since left the United States.[4] While this alleged incident involved a potential violation of U.S. antitrafficking laws, abuse allegations by household workers against foreign diplomats have ranged from potential wage and hour violations to involuntary servitude. For the purposes of this report, we will use the term abuse to include all such allegations.

Most of the household workers brought to the United States by foreign diplomats arrive with A-3 visas—as employees of officials from foreign embassies, consulates, or governments—or with G-5 visas—as employees of foreign officials for international organizations, such as the United Nations or the World Bank.[5] On average, almost 3,500 individuals enter the United States each year on A-3 and G-5 visas. Several U.S. government agencies are involved in efforts to respond to alleged abuse of these visa holders. State grants A-3 and G-5 visas, issues guidance on diplomatic law, and maintains official records regarding the status and immunity level of foreign diplomats in the United States, among other things. The Department of Justice (Justice) investigates trafficking allegations and prosecutes violations of criminal statutes. The Department of Homeland Security (Homeland Security) investigates trafficking allegations and grants T visas to some trafficking victims. These visas allow victims to remain in the United States for up to 4 years, file for permanent residence, and receive certain government services through the Department of Health and Human Services. The Department of Labor (Labor) investigates allegations of wage and hour violations.

In response to your request, we (1) sought to determine how many A-3 and G-5 visa holders have alleged abuse by foreign diplomats with immunity since 2000, (2) reviewed the U.S. government's process for investigating abuse allegations involving foreign diplomats with immunity, and (3) described and assessed how State ensures correct and consistent implementation of A-3 and G-5 visa policies and procedures.

To determine how many A-3 and G-5 visa holders have alleged abuse by foreign diplomats with immunity, we interviewed U.S. government officials and analyzed data provided by these officials on alleged incidents that they have handled. We requested data on alleged incidents that occurred from calendar years 2000 through 2008. We also met with representatives of 10 nongovernmental organizations (NGOs) that provide services to alleged victims of abuse by foreign diplomats and analyzed data they provided on allegations. In addition, we conducted legal research to identify relevant civil lawsuits. To review the U.S. government's process for investigating allegations, we analyzed State's policies for handling allegations of criminal activity by foreign diplomats and interviewed U.S. government officials. To describe and assess how State ensures correct and consistent implementation of A-3 and G-5 visa policies and procedures, we analyzed State's guidance and requirements for adjudicating these visas, and interviewed State officials. We also met with consular officers and reviewed A-3 and G-5 visa files at the U.S. embassies in Peru, the Philippines, Qatar, and Saudi Arabia. We assessed the reliability of data analyzed and found them to be sufficiently reliable for purposes of this report. We conducted this performance audit between October 2007 and July 2008 in accordance with generally accepted government auditing standards. Those standards require that we plan and perform the audit to obtain sufficient, appropriate evidence to provide a reasonable basis for our findings and conclusions based on our audit objectives. We believe that the evidence obtained provides a reasonable basis for our findings and conclusions based on our audit objectives. (App. I provides a detailed discussion of our objectives, scope, and methodology.)

RESULTS IN BRIEF

We identified 42 distinct A-3 and G-5 visa holders who alleged that they were abused by foreign diplomats with some level of immunity from 2000 through 2008, but the total number of alleged incidents is likely higher. The 42 alleged incidents we confirmed include those identified by federal agencies, NGOs, and legal sources, such as Westlaw. Ten of these alleged incidents resulted in federal human trafficking investigations, most of which remain open. In one instance, Justice determined through its investigation that, absent immunity, it would indict the foreign diplomat's wife. However, the diplomat's home government declined to waive the wife's immunity; thus, Justice could not indict. The diplomat and his wife subsequently left the United States. The total number of alleged incidents of household worker abuse by foreign diplomats with some level of immunity is likely higher than the 42 distinct alleged incidents we have identified for four reasons: household workers' fear of contacting law enforcement authorities, NGOs' need to maintain client confidentiality, limited information on some allegations handled by the U.S. government, and federal agencies' difficulties in tracking household worker abuse allegations and investigations involving foreign diplomats. For example, the *Foreign Affairs Manual* [6] states that several offices and bureaus within State will provide the Office of Protocol and the Office of the Legal Adviser with reports on all cases that come to their attention, but we found that these offices were not aware of all cases that had been handled by the department. In addition, law enforcement agencies were unable to search their case management databases for investigations involving foreign diplomats because these databases are not designed to track investigations in this manner.

The U.S. government's process for investigating allegations of abuse by foreign diplomats is complicated by three factors: (1) constraints imposed by immunity, (2) household workers' heightened vulnerabilities due to their employers' status, and (3) the length of time it takes for Justice to obtain State's opinion on the use of certain investigative techniques in trafficking investigations involving individuals with varying degrees of immunity and inviolability. Law enforcement's ability to investigate foreign diplomats is limited, particularly if the subject has full immunity or inviolable premises are involved. Diplomats with full immunity have the highest degree of privileges and immunities. They are considered "personally inviolable" and cannot be detained. In addition, their residences are inviolable and cannot be entered or searched without their consent. These limitations are particularly challenging because abuse of household workers typically takes place in the employer's residence and often is not witnessed by individuals outside the employer's family. Furthermore, the victims may not cooperate out of fear that the employers will use their political status and connections to harm them or their families or that they will be deported if they leave their employment situations. Finally, while Justice consults with State to identify investigative techniques that can be used when foreign diplomats have immunity, some recent consultations have taken several months because, according to State and Justice officials, they raised unprecedented questions. Law enforcement officials told us that these lengthy consultations can hamper investigations. Justice would like for State to clarify which techniques are not legally permissible when the subject of the investigation has full or partial immunity but, according to State officials, State prefers to handle these investigations on a case-by-case basis so that it can consider fully the legal and policy implications of each case. State considers the extent to which its opinion on the permissibility of a given technique could be defended legally. State also reviews each case through the lens of reciprocity—assessing how U.S. diplomats abroad might be affected by actions taken toward a foreign diplomat on U.S. soil. While Justice and State agree that it would be helpful to outline an interagency process for communicating in a timely manner about the use of investigative techniques in these cases, they have, thus far, not taken any formal steps to create one.

At the four consular posts we visited, we found weaknesses in State's process for ensuring that its policies for issuing A-3 and G-5 visas are implemented correctly and consistently, and some consular officers were unfamiliar with or unclear about aspects of guidance relating to these visas. Our review of employment contracts submitted by A-3 and G-5 visa applicants at the posts we visited showed that, in many cases, they did not include some or all of the criteria required in the *Foreign Affairs Manual*, such as a guarantee that the employee will receive the minimum or prevailing wage (whichever is greater).[7] Some consular officers we spoke with also were unaware of or unclear about aspects of State's general guidance on A-3 and G-5 visas. For example, several consular officers did not know that, according to State guidance, they should keep electronically scanned copies of the employment contracts on file. Consular officers also were uncertain about the reasons for refusing A-3 or G-5 visas. State's guidance directs consular officers to determine that A-3 and G-5 visa applicants are entering into true employer-employee relationships, in accordance with required terms of their personal employment contracts, but does not explicitly state whether concerns about abuse or mistreatment are sufficient grounds on which to refuse an A-3 or G-5 visa. At one post, officers told us that they can refuse an A-3 or G-5 visa if they believe that the worker may not be treated well. However, officers at two other posts said that it can be very difficult to refuse an A-3 or G-5 visa, even if they believe that the worker will be underpaid or treated poorly, particularly if they lack hard evidence that an applicant has been or could be mistreated. State headquarters officials currently do not alert consular officers if they have information linking a particular foreign diplomat to a pattern of abuse allegations. State is considering steps to clarify its guidance, such as directing consular officers to refuse A-3 or G-5 visas if there is a pattern of past alleged abuse by a particular diplomat, but has not set a time frame for doing so. In addition, State headquarters does not exercise oversight by periodically assessing compliance with A-3 and G-5 visa policies and procedures, but instead relies on individual posts to do so.

In this report, we recommend that the Secretary of State (1) emphasize to the relevant bureaus and offices the importance of the *Foreign Affairs Manual* requirement to report all cases that come to their attention and create a system for collecting and maintaining records on these cases, (2) work with the Attorney General of the United States and the Secretary of Homeland Security to establish an interagency process outlining agreed-upon policies and time frames for determining which investigative techniques can be used in trafficking investigations involving foreign diplomats, (3) establish a system alerting consular officers to seek guidance from State headquarters before issuing A-3 or G-5 visas to applicants whose prospective employers may have abused their household workers in the past, and (4) enhance oversight by establishing a monitoring system to spot-check compliance with A-3 and G-5 visa policies and procedures.

The Departments of State and Justice provided written comments on a draft of our report, which are reprinted in appendixes IV and V, respectively.

State concurred with all four of our recommendations. Regarding the first recommendation, State indicated that it will emphasize to the relevant bureaus and offices the importance of reporting promptly and fully all cases of alleged abuse. State also noted that the Office of Protocol has begun creating a system for collecting and maintaining centralized records on these cases. With regard to our second recommendation, State noted that it will be useful to establish a process to address novel and difficult questions regarding investigative techniques. In response to our third recommendation, State said that it will proactively "watch-list" known abusers in its Consular Lookout and Support System and will soon provide consular officers improved information regarding A-3 and G-5 cases. Finally, State acknowledged the need for better compliance with A-3 and G-5 visa policies and procedures and agreed to consider our fourth recommendation to spot-check compliance from headquarters.

Justice agreed with our findings and concurred with our second recommendation, noting that agreeing upon time frames for deciding on the use of investigative techniques is particularly important.

In addition, State, Justice, and Homeland Security provided technical comments on a draft of our report, which we incorporated as appropriate. For example, Homeland Security asked to be included in our second recommendation, which initially was directed to the Secretary of State and the Attorney General. We agreed to amend the recommendation accordingly.

The Departments of Labor and Health and Human Services chose not to comment on the draft report.

BACKGROUND

Each year, State issues A-3 and G-5 visas to individuals whose employers are foreign diplomats on official purposes in the United States.[8] Most of these individuals are hired to work for foreign diplomats in the District of Columbia, Maryland, New York, or Virginia. For fiscal years 2000 through 2007, 207 U.S. embassies and consular posts overseas issued 10,386 A-3 visas and 7,522 G-5 visas. The number of A-3 visas decreased[9] during this period by about 56 percent—from 1,780 in fiscal year 2000 to 999 in fiscal year 2007—and the number of G-5 visas issued increased by 21 percent— from 877 in fiscal year 2000 to 1,057 in fiscal year 2007 (see fig. 1).

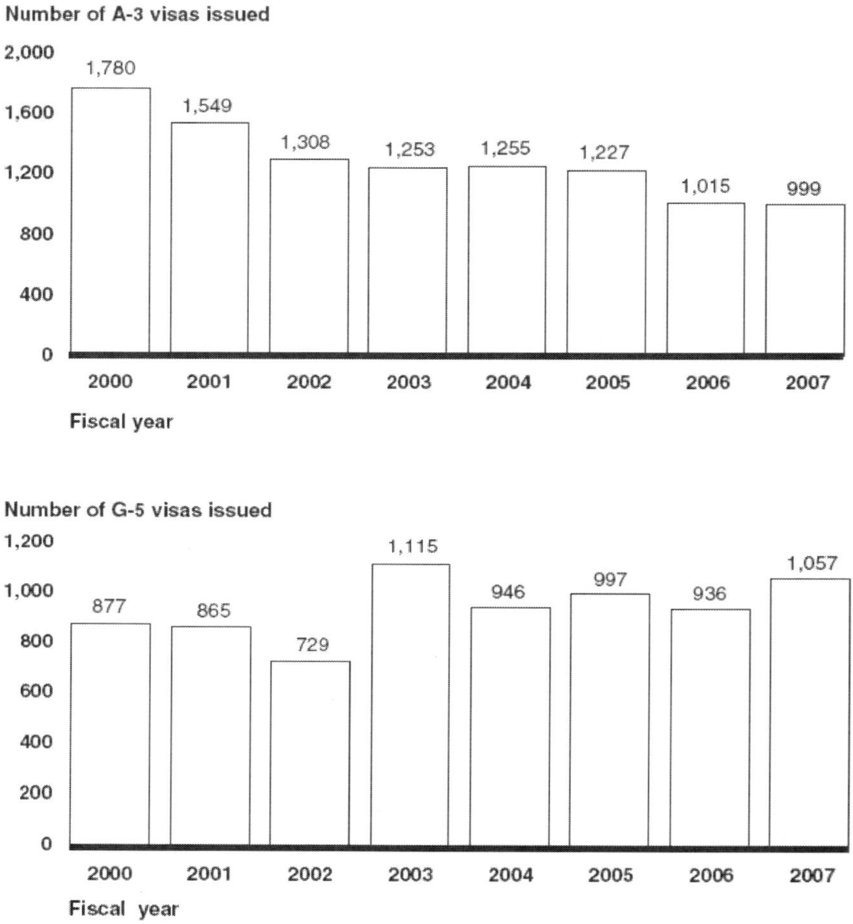

Source: GAO analysis of State data.

Figure 1. Number of A3 and G-5 Visas Issued Abroad, Fiscal Years 2000 to 2007.

Figure 2 shows the 10 posts that issued the most A-3 and G-5 visas, combined, for fiscal years 2000 through 2007. These 10 posts issued 40 percent of the total number of A-3 and G-5 visas issued during this period. Manila issued the most A-3 and G-5 visas, accounting for almost 10 percent of the total number of these visas issued overseas during this period.

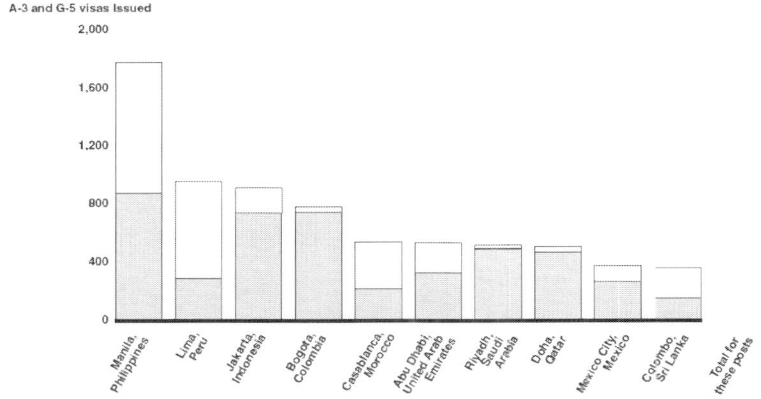

	Manila, Philippines	Lima, Peru	Jakarta, Indonesia	Bogota, Colombia	Casablanca, Morocco	Abu Dhabi, United Arab Emirates	Riyadh, Saudi Arabia	Doha, Qatar	Mexico City, Mexico	Colombo, Sri Lanka	Total for these posts
Percentage of total at overseas posts	9.9%	5.3%	5.1%	4.3%	3.0%	2.9%	2.8%	2.0%	2.0%	2.0%	40.3%
A-3 and G-5 total visas issued	1,775	956	910	778	531	528	509	502	367	355	7,211
G-5 visas issued	904	675	173	36	322	206	22	38	108	211	2,695
A-3 visas issued	871	281	737	742	209	322	487	464	259	144	4,516

Source: GAO analysis of State data.

Figure 2. Overseas Posts that Issued the Most A-3 and G-5 Visas, Fiscal Years 2000 to 2007.

U.S. laws provide certain protections for household workers, including individuals brought to the United States on A-3 or G-5 visas, and State, Justice, Homeland Security, and Labor work to respond to allegations of abuse, exploitation, or trafficking of household workers by foreign diplomats. (App. II lists the relevant offices within these departments and their respective responsibilities.) The U.S. government considers involuntary servitude of household workers, as defined under the Trafficking Victims Protection Act of 2000, to be a severe form of trafficking in persons and a serious criminal offense. Specifically, the act defines severe forms of trafficking in persons, in part, as the recruitment, harboring, transportation, provision, or maintaining of a person for labor or services through the use of force, fraud, or coercion for the purpose of subjection to involuntary servitude, peonage, debt bondage, or slavery. Victims of severe forms of trafficking are offered certain accommodations under the act. Household workers also are subject to U.S. laws and covered by the Fair Labor Standards Act, which is the law governing minimum wages and overtime pay. Homeland Security can provide special accommodations to individuals who show that their employers have abused, exploited, or trafficked them, allowing the workers to legally remain in the United States. These accommodations are continued presence[10]—which permits an alien to be present legally in the United States and to seek work during the investigation—and T nonimmigrant status[11]—which permits a visa holder to remain in the United States for up to 4 years, file for adjustment of status to lawful permanent residence, and apply for benefits from the U.S. government such as food stamps and medical assistance. If they leave their employment situation without either of these accommodations, A-3 and G-5 visa holders lose their legal immigration status and could be deported.

Under international and domestic law, the U.S. government, including its law enforcement authorities, extends privileges and immunities to certain foreign diplomats.[12] Employers of A-3 and G-5 visa holders may be entitled to some degree of immunity (full or partial) or may have no immunity at all. An employer with full diplomatic immunity is generally immune from civil or criminal jurisdiction of U.S. courts. Certain employers with partial or "official acts" immunity, such as most individuals employed by international organizations, are immune from civil or criminal jurisdiction of U.S. courts for conduct performed under their official duties or functions. State and the United Nations publish lists of current foreign diplomats who hold diplomatic rank[13] on their Web sites. Appendix III identifies the respective privileges and immunities to which various categories of foreign diplomats are entitled.

42 A-3 and G-5 Visa Holders Have Alleged Abuse Since 2000; Total Number of Alleged Incidents Is Likely Higher

We identified 42 individual A-3 and G-5 visa holders who have alleged abuse by foreign diplomats with some level of immunity in the United States from 2000 through June 2008. However, the total number of alleged incidents is likely to be higher for four reasons: household workers' fear of contacting law enforcement authorities, NGOs' protection of victim confidentiality, limited information on some allegations handled by the U.S. government, and federal departments' difficulties in tracking household worker abuse allegations and investigations involving foreign diplomats.

GAO Identified 42 A-3 and G-5 Visa Holders Who Have Alleged Abuse Since 2000

We identified 42 distinct A-3 or G-5 visa holders who, since 2000, have alleged that foreign diplomats[14] with some level of immunity abused them.[15] We confirmed that 17 of the incidents alleged by these A-3 or G-5 visa holders were handled by federal agencies.[16] These 17 incidents[17] can be categorized as follows:

- 10 alleged incidents of human trafficking, which resulted in eight human trafficking investigations;[18]
- one investigation of alleged visa fraud;[19]
- one investigation of an alleged wage and hour violation; and
- five alleged incidents identified by State, some of which may have resulted in investigations, including
- one human trafficking allegation;
- two allegations of physical or verbal abuse; and
- two alleged wage and hour violations.

Most of the human trafficking investigations remain open. However, in one of the human trafficking investigations, Justice determined that, absent immunity, it would indict the foreign diplomat's wife. State requested that the diplomat's home government waive immunity, which would allow Justice to indict her. However, the diplomat's home government declined to waive immunity; thus, Justice could not indict. The diplomat and his wife subsequently left the United States, and Justice has since closed this case.

We identified the remaining 25 distinct alleged incidents through legal sources, such as Westlaw, and interviews with NGOs who provided services to the alleged victims, such as assistance in applying for T visas and filing lawsuits against their employers. According to NGOs, 4 of these 25 alleged victims applied for and received T visas. In addition, we determined that civil suits were filed in 9 of these 25 alleged incidents. In most of these lawsuits, household workers sought, in part, to recoup unpaid wages. According to NGOs, the courts dismissed three of the nine lawsuits on the basis that the foreign diplomats had immunity.[20] Of the remaining six lawsuits, NGOs indicated that five were settled out of court, and one resulted in a default judgment because the defendants failed to respond. Although we could not confirm that any of these 25 alleged incidents were investigated or handled by the U.S. government, NGOs told us that they reported 12 of them to federal agencies. They did not report the other 13 alleged incidents.

Number of Alleged Incidents Likely Higher than the 42 We Identified

The total number of alleged incidents of household employee abuse by foreign diplomats with some level of immunity is likely to exceed the total we have identified for four reasons. First, as we have previously reported, trafficking victims are a hidden population because trafficking is a clandestine activity.[21] Trafficking victims often are in a precarious position and may be unwilling or unable to report to, or seek help from, relevant authorities. Moreover, the Department of Health and Human Services reported that victims live daily with inhumane treatment, physical and mental abuse, and threats to themselves or their families back home. Victims of human trafficking may fear or distrust the government and police because they are afraid of being deported or because they come from countries where law enforcement is corrupt and feared. In such circumstances, reporting to the police or seeking help elsewhere requires courage and knowledge of local conditions, which the victims might not have. In addition, some victims may not be permitted to leave their employers' residences, which makes it much more difficult to report their abuse to authorities.

Second, NGOs have provided services to alleged victims who did not want to be identified or who did not want to identify their employers. NGOs we contacted told us that, since 2000, they have received allegations from 66 A-3 or G-5 visa holders stating that they were abused by their employers. However, in 31 of these alleged incidents, the worker and the diplomat involved were not identified either because the worker was too afraid to reveal his or her identity or because the organization agreed to protect the client's confidentiality.

Third, because of federal agencies' need to protect sensitive information, we received limited data on some alleged incidents handled by the U.S. government, and thus did not include those incidents in our total count. In most instances, federal agencies did not reveal the names or countries of origin of the worker and foreign diplomat involved in alleged incidents they had investigated or otherwise handled. It is law enforcement policy not to disclose details of ongoing criminal investigations. Without this information, however, we could not fully reflect federal agencies' data in our overall count of alleged incidents without potentially double counting ones that had already been reported to us by NGOs. For example, although Justice told us of 19 human trafficking investigations involving foreign diplomats with immunity, we could only confirm that 8 of them were included in our count of 42 distinct alleged incidents. Justice officials also told us that there are likely multiple victims in some of the 19 trafficking investigations they reported to us. Furthermore, while Homeland Security identified nine A-3 and G-5 visa holders who received T visas from Homeland Security's Citizenship and Immigration Services, we did not learn the names of their employers, and therefore could not confirm if they held immunity.

Fourth, federal officials said they could not determine definitively the total number of alleged incidents they had handled and could only estimate that number by reviewing specific case files and consulting with knowledgeable staff. Officials had difficulty identifying all alleged incidents or investigations in their records or databases for several reasons as explained below:

- Justice, Immigration and Customs Enforcement, and Diplomatic Security officials could not identify all investigations because their databases are not designed or meant to facilitate searches based on characteristics of the alleged perpetrators, such as whether they are foreign diplomats.
- Justice officials told us that the ongoing investigations they identified, primarily by canvassing knowledgeable staff, only went back as far as May 2005.
- In addition, Immigration and Customs Enforcement could not identify investigations before 2003, because it had difficulties capturing traffickingin-persons data prior to its creation as part of Homeland Security in that year.[22]
- State has several offices that receive allegations of abuse by foreign diplomats, but no single office maintains information on all allegations. According to the *Foreign Affairs Manual*, the Office of Protocol establishes and maintains complete records of each reported case that comes to its attention in which a foreign diplomat with immunity from criminal jurisdiction has been accused of a crime in the United States. State defines "accused of a crime" to mean cases in which Justice has determined that, absent immunity, it would seek to indict. Therefore, although the Office of Protocol receives reports of allegations from other federal agencies,[23] other State bureaus and offices, and some NGOs, it does not systematically maintain records

on other ongoing criminal investigations, civil lawsuits that have been filed, or any other allegations. Moreover, the *Foreign Affairs Manual* indicates that State's Bureau of International Organizations, the U.S. Mission to the United Nations (USUN), each regional bureau, and Diplomatic Security will provide the Office of Protocol and the Office of the Legal Adviser with reports on all cases that come to their attention. However, there is no mechanism to ensure that these reports are referred to and recorded by the Office of Protocol and the Office of the Legal Adviser. We found that the Office of Protocol was unaware of cases that USUN had handled, and the Office of Protocol and the Office of the Legal Adviser were unaware of all cases that Diplomatic Security had handled.

- While Labor's system tracks the 30,000 to 40,000 investigations of alleged wage and hour violations it conducts each year, it does not specifically identify those involving foreign diplomats. In addition, although Justice and Homeland Security officials told us they have referred allegations of wage and hour violations to Labor, they could not identify the specific allegations. Labor officials told us that they were aware only of one investigation of an alleged wage and hour violation, but that policy is for field offices to inform headquarters of any allegations of wage and hour violations received involving foreign diplomats.

THREE FACTORS COMPLICATE INVESTIGATIONS OF ABUSE BY FOREIGN DIPLOMATS

The U.S. government's process of investigating foreign diplomats for alleged abuse is complicated by three factors—(1) constraints posed by immunity, (2) household workers' heightened vulnerabilities due to their employers' status, and (3) the length of time it takes for Justice to obtain State's opinion on the use of specific investigative techniques in trafficking investigations.

Immunity Poses Constraints for Investigations

When investigating foreign diplomats with immunity, law enforcement agents face constraints that become particularly pronounced when the alleged crime has taken place in the diplomat's residence. Investigators' options are most limited when a diplomat has full immunity and is considered to have personal inviolability or when the diplomat's residence is considered inviolable. Diplomats who are personally inviolable cannot be detained, and property that is considered inviolable (including vehicles and residences) cannot be entered or searched without the diplomats' consent. Although the residences of foreign diplomats with partial immunity may be searched, these diplomats cannot be obliged to give evidence concerning matters related to their official duties.

Officials at Justice, Homeland Security, and the Federal Bureau of Investigation (FBI) told us that these limitations pose particular problems when the allegation involves abuse of a household employee because the worker's mistreatment often occurs in the employer's residence and is not witnessed by individuals outside the employer's family. For example, a Justice official told us that these allegations can be among the most difficult to investigate and prosecute because it is hard for investigators to gather enough corroborating evidence. Investigators are prohibited from observing working and living conditions in the home absent the diplomat's consent, and possible witnesses often include the diplomat's family, who also may have immunity. Instead, investigators often have to rely primarily on interviewing the victim and talking to neighbors who may have observed interactions between the diplomat and the household employee. In some instances, the evidence collected through these methods is considered insufficient to pursue prosecution. These constraints resulted in at least one instance in which law enforcement officials closed an investigation for lack of sufficient evidence after they determined that constraints posed by immunity prevented investigators from talking to witnesses inside a foreign diplomat's home.

Diplomats' Status Heightens Workers' Vulnerabilities

The status of foreign diplomats under investigation can heighten their household workers' sense of vulnerability. For example, household workers may be intimidated by their employers' wealth, political connections, or prominent positions in society. One Justice official told us that abusive situations involving foreign diplomats' household workers have a striking power imbalance because workers often are poor, uneducated, and fear retaliation, not only against themselves but also against family members in their home country. This fear can inhibit household workers from cooperating with investigations, further limiting the investigators' options for collecting evidence. NGOs told us that foreign diplomats have used immunity as a weapon to frighten their household workers and discourage them from escaping or taking actions to improve their situation. Workers have alleged that their employers threatened their family members back home, told them they would be deported if they did not do as they were instructed, and stated they could treat them as they chose because immunity allows them to do so with impunity. As reported above, we also learned from some NGOs of a number of allegations of household worker abuse by foreign diplomats that were not reported to the U.S. government because the workers were too afraid of potential consequences. In these instances, an investigation could not even be initiated.

Lengthy Process for Determining the Permissibility of Using Investigative Techniques Can Hamper Trafficking Investigations

Justice requests State's advice on how diplomatic immunity impacts the legal permissibility of using certain investigative techniques, but the time-consuming process of obtaining State's opinion can hamper investigations. When Justice receives an allegation that a foreign diplomat has abused a household worker, it reviews the facts and determines if they merit opening a trafficking investigation. If Justice decides to open an investigation (or learns that Immigration and Customs Enforcement or the FBI has opened a new investigation), it contacts State to (1) confirm the diplomat's identity and level of immunity; (2) determine how State wants to be kept informed of the investigation; and (3) obtain State's opinion, if necessary, on the use of certain investigative techniques. State officials said that there is no formal requirement for Justice to consult with them on whether certain investigative techniques are permissible, but that it is appropriate and they welcome Justice to do so. According to Justice, because U.S. courts take into account State's interpretation of international treaties and conventions, Justice requests State's legal interpretation on these matters. Although certain techniques, such as searching the residence of a diplomat who has full immunity and inviolability without the diplomat's consent, are clearly prohibited, other techniques may touch the diplomat's "sphere of privacy." According to State officials, the permissibility of these techniques under international law is less clear.[24]

While State can readily confirm a diplomat's identity, State's process of advising on which investigative techniques are legally permissible has, in some instances involving unprecedented circumstances, taken several months. In one instance, a victim agreed to a specific investigative technique that could have allowed Justice to collect important evidence. The victim's lawyers postponed filing a civil suit on her behalf to avoid alerting the diplomat involved that he was under investigation. State spent 6 months deliberating the issue, but did not advise Justice on whether use of this technique was legally permissible. Justice did not use the technique, the victim's lawyers eventually filed suit, and the criminal investigation remains open. In other instances, State has asked Justice to provide specific information that it believes could help it formulate an opinion on whether use of the technique is legally permissible. According to a Justice official, obtaining some of this information can be difficult and time-consuming. Both Justice and State officials agreed that when the issue at hand is relatively straightforward, they reach agreement quickly.

According to State, its internal process of reaching an opinion on the legal advisability of investigative techniques can be time-consuming because State takes both legal and policy considerations into account when considering the advisability of using investigative techniques that fall into the "gray area." For example, the involvement of foreign diplomats can raise sensitivities for the U.S. government. State may need to consider reciprocity, such as how use of a specific technique might affect treatment of U.S. diplomats abroad. Similarly, if the foreign diplomat's country is a close ally of the United States, State also will assess how relations with that country might be affected by use of the investigative technique. The process of addressing these questions through State's supervisory chain of command, which can go above the Assistant Secretary level, if necessary, is lengthy, according to State officials. Once State makes a final determination, a State official conveys to a Justice official the department's opinion on use of the investigative technique in the specific case. This opinion covers both State's legal determination and any policy concerns the department may have. For example, a State official might say that the department could probably defend the use of a technique legally, but it would raise serious reciprocity concerns.

According to Justice, State's policy considerations do not affect its trafficking investigations, but the length of State's deliberative process in determining what is legally permissible can hamper them. The investigative techniques in question are, according to Justice officials, among the most useful for gathering corroborating evidence, but they are unlikely to succeed unless they are implemented quickly. As one Justice official explained, "time is the enemy of successful investigations," meaning that the longer it takes to get approval from State, the greater the likelihood that the investigation will be compromised. For example, the subjects might learn that they are under investigation or they might leave the United States for their next assignment, further limiting the opportunity to collect evidence. Homeland Security officials also told us that any delays are detrimental to the preservation and collection of physical and testimonial evidence.

To expedite the investigative process, Justice officials said that it would be helpful for State to provide them with a list of investigative techniques that, in State's view, are not legally permissible when the subject of the investigation has full or partial immunity. However, State prefers to continue handling these investigations on a case-by-case basis. State officials explained that, while they could make a list of techniques that are clearly acceptable (such as asking the diplomat to agree to an interview) or prohibited (such as searching the residence of a diplomat with full immunity and inviolability), they would rather not indicate the legal permissibility of other, less clear-cut techniques because they want to be able to consider both the legal and policy implications of each case. However, these officials added that they are aware of the need to provide a more timely response to Justice. Officials from both agencies told us they are considering developing an interagency process that would outline time frames for discussing the use of investigative techniques, but they have, thus far, not taken any formal actions toward creating one.

Weaknesses Exist in Implementation and Oversight of A-3 and G-5 Visa Policies and Procedures

At the four consular posts we visited, we found weaknesses in State's process for ensuring that its policies for issuing A-3 and G-5 visas are implemented correctly and consistently, and some consular officers were unfamiliar with or unclear about aspects of guidance relating to these visas. Although State headquarters issues A-3 and G-5 policies and procedures, it relies on individual posts to ensure they are implemented correctly and consistently and has not instituted a process to spot-check compliance.

GAO Found Weaknesses in the Implementation of A-3 and G-5 Visa Policies

Through our fieldwork, we identified instances in which A-3 and G-5 policies were not implemented correctly and consistently. State requires that A-3 and G-5 visa applicants submit employment contracts signed by both the employer and employee that include

- a guarantee that the employee will be compensated at the state or federal minimum wage or prevailing wage, whichever is greater;
- a statement by the employee that he or she will not accept any other employment while working for the employer;
- a statement by the employer that he or she will not withhold the passport of the employee; and
- a statement indicating that both parties understand that the employee cannot be required to remain on the premises after working hours without compensation.

However, the contracts we reviewed[25] did not include at least one of State's requirements 71 percent of the time at one post, 35 percent at the second, 23 percent at the third, and 6 percent at the fourth.[26]

- In some cases, the contracts were clearly deficient in one or more areas. For example, one contract we reviewed showed that the employee would receive $5 per hour (below the minimum wage) and that the employee would reimburse her employer for items received. This particular contract also did not include a statement that the employee could not be required to remain on the premises after working hours without compensation.
- In other cases, the contracts included statements that appeared to comply with State's requirements, but also contained information that contradicted these statements. For example, some contracts stated that "the normal working hours of the second party [employee] shall be at the prevailing wage for a 40 hours [sic] week." However, these contracts also showed that the employees would be paid well below the prevailing wage for their occupation and intended destination.

Our review of employment contracts revealed other shortcomings and raised questions about whether the employee would be paid fairly.

- A-3 and G-5 visa applicants must submit contracts in English and a language understood by the applicants to demonstrate they understand their duties and rights regarding salary and working conditions. However, at one post where consular officers told us that A-3 and G-5 visa applicants rarely speak or read English, none of the contracts we reviewed was in a language other than English.[27]
- We identified some contracts where the employee would be paid overtime "in accordance with [the foreign diplomat's home] embassy regulations."
- In another contract, the employee's overtime hourly rate was lower than her wage for normal working hours.

Some Consular Officers Unfamiliar with or Unclear about Aspects of A-3 and G-5 Policies and Procedures

At the four posts we visited, we also found that some consular officers were unfamiliar with or unclear about certain aspects of State's guidance on A-3 and G-5 visas.

Requiring a Diplomatic Note

According to State's guidance, A-3 and G-5 visa applications must be accompanied by a diplomatic note from the appropriate foreign mission or international organization that identifies the applicant's employer and confirms the employer's official A or G status. Some consular officers overseas told us that they believed a note was not required if they could identify the employer and confirm his or her status through The Office of Foreign Missions Information System (TOMIS), a database of foreign diplomats posted to the United States, which, according to the *Foreign Affairs Manual*, can be a useful tool for consular officers to confirm a diplomat's status. However, senior consular officials at State headquarters told us that TOMIS may contain inaccurate or outdated information and confirmed that a diplomatic note was in fact required.

Informing A-3 and G-5 Visa Applicants of Their Rights

State's guidance also includes provisions encouraging consular officers to help educate A-3 and G-5 visa applicants about their rights under U.S. laws, but some officers we spoke with were unaware of these provisions. Consular officers are required to interview all A-3 and G-5 visa applicants. State recommends that officers use the interview to advise applicants in a language they understand that the U.S. government considers involuntary servitude of household workers to be a severe form of trafficking in persons and a serious criminal offense and that victims of involuntary servitude are offered protection under the Trafficking Victims Protection Act. Officers are encouraged to make A-3 and G-5 applicants aware that the telephone number for police and emergency services is 911, and that there is a telephone hotline for reporting abuse of household workers and other trafficking-related crimes.[28] State also reminds consular posts that an antitrafficking brochure titled "Be Smart, Be Safe" is available as a handout to household worker applicants. However, while several officers said they try to explain to A-3 and G-5 visa applicants that they have rights under U.S. laws, the officers also were unaware of the telephone hotline, State's advice to refer workers to 911, or the brochure. None of the posts we visited made copies of the "Be Smart, Be Safe" brochure available to visa applicants, although two of them had created one-page informational handouts for A-3 and G-5 visa applicants.[29] At one of these posts, officers generally did not speak with applicants about their rights but instead relied on giving them the one-page handout. NGOs and alleged victims we spoke with told us that measures to educate A-3 and G-5 visa applicants are important. For example, one alleged victim said that U.S. embassies abroad should tell domestic workers coming to the United States that they have rights because, in her experience, one of the ways that employers abuse their workers is to tell them that they are still under the laws of their home country. She added that, specifically, embassies should give A-3 and G-5 visa applicants information about whom to contact if they experience physical or psychological abuse. Another worker, whose employer was investigated and sent home for allegedly trafficking household workers, told her attorneys that she knew to seek help because a consular officer had told her about her rights under U.S. law when she applied for her A-3 visa.

Scanning Employment Contracts

Another area of the guidance that posts we visited were largely unaware of was the March 2007 direction from State headquarters to electronically scan copies of A-3 and G-5 employment contracts into the Consular Consolidated Database, which contains information on visa applicants. Two of the posts we visited had not scanned any of their contracts into the database, one had scanned about half of the contracts we reviewed, and the remaining one had only scanned a few. A State official in Washington explained that scanning documents is useful because, in cases of alleged abuse, accessing a copy of the contract provides evidence that the diplomat had agreed to provide better working conditions.[30] NGOs also emphasized the importance of being able to access employment contracts. For example, an NGO told us that in one case, a foreign diplomat gave his worker a contract to present when applying for a G-5 visa that said that she would receive $1,200 per month, but gave her a different contract when she arrived in the United States that said she would receive only $425 per month. The organization is now trying to locate a copy of the original contract.

Criteria for Refusing A-3 and G-5 Visas

Finally, consular officers at the posts we visited were uncertain about the reasons for which they could refuse A-3 and G-5 visas. State's guidance directs consular officers to determine that A-3 and G-5 visa applicants are entering into true employer-employee relationships, in accordance with required terms of their personal employment contracts. However, it does not explicitly state if concerns about abuse or mistreatment are sufficient grounds on which to refuse an A-3 or G-5 visa. At one post we visited, consular officers told us they were comfortable refusing these visas, particularly if there were indications that the worker might not be treated well. They might refuse the visa if the applicant was under age 18 or if the employer resisted requests by the consular officers to interview the applicant alone. In an attempt to ensure better treatment of household workers, that post instituted a policy of preferring individuals to have worked for the sponsoring diplomat for 1 year before applying for an A-3 visa.[31] While the consular officers at this post said they believed they had considerable latitude to refuse A-3 or G-5 visas, other officers we spoke with said that they did not. For example, the Deputy Chief of Mission at one post told us that he "wished he could refuse more A-3 and G-5 visas," but that he was unsure of consular officers' ability to deny A-3 and G-5 visa applicants. Several consular officers echoed these comments, noting that, without hard evidence that an applicant has been or could be mistreated, it is difficult to deny an A-3 or G-5 visa. For example, a consular officer at one post we visited told us that, in one case, she was concerned that the applicant had never met her employer, but her supervisors told her that as long as the applicant had a valid employment contract, she had to issue the visa.

State is considering steps to address confusion about refusing A-3 and G-5 visas, but has not taken actions to implement them. Consular officials in Washington told us that, while it is appropriate and even expected for consular officers to refuse A-3 and G-5 visas if they believe that visa applicants may be abused by their prospective employers, the officers have "little to go on department, we recommend that the Secretary of State (1) emphasize to the relevant bureaus and offices the importance of the *Foreign Affairs Manual* requirement to report all cases that come to their attention and (2) direct the Office of Protocol and the Office of the Legal Adviser to create a system for collecting and maintaining records on these cases.

2) To assist in timely handling of future investigations, we recommend that the Secretary of State, the Attorney General, and the Secretary of Homeland Security establish an interagency process outlining agreed-upon policies and time frames for determining which investigative techniques can be used in trafficking investigations involving foreign diplomats.
3) We recommend that the Secretary of State direct the Bureau of Consular Affairs, in coordination with the Office of Protocol and the Office of the Legal Adviser, to establish a system alerting consular officers to seek guidance from State headquarters before issuing A-3 or G-5 visas to applicants whose prospective employers may have abused their household workers in the past. For example, if State headquarters is aware that a foreign diplomat is under investigation for alleged human trafficking, it could place an alert in the system advising consular officers to request guidance should an individual apply for an A-3 or G-5 visa to work for that diplomat.
4) To better ensure correct and consistent implementation of A-3 and G-5 visa policies and procedures, particularly those that outline requirements for employment contracts, we recommend that the Secretary of State enhance oversight by establishing a system to spot-check compliance with these policies and procedures. This spot-check system would allow headquarters to assess compliance without dedicating the resources needed to review all A-3 and G-5 visas issued in a given year and could be targeted at posts that issue high numbers of A-3 or G-5 visas or that have identified difficulties interpreting guidance on these visas classes.

Agency Comments and Our Evaluation

We provided a draft of this report to the Departments of State, Justice, Homeland Security, Labor, and Health and Human Services for their comments. State and Justice provided written comments on the draft, which we have reprinted in appendixes IV and V, respectively.

State agreed with all four of our recommendations. Regarding the first recommendation, State indicated that it will emphasize to the relevant bureaus and offices the importance of reporting promptly and fully all cases of alleged abuse of household workers by foreign diplomats. State also noted that the Office of Protocol is now creating a system for collecting and maintaining centralized records on these cases that would allow for ready access to records of cases that involve individuals with immunity. Regarding our second recommendation, State said that, while most investigations go forward without consultations on investigative techniques, it will be useful to establish a process to address novel and difficult questions regarding investigative techniques. In response to our third recommendation, State said that it will place known abusers of household workers in the Consular Lookout and Support System, a database designed to screen visa applicants and maintain watch lists. State will also upgrade consular officers' access to TOMIS to provide improved information regarding A-3 and G-5 cases. State responded to our last recommendation by acknowledging the need for better compliance with policies and procedures to ensure that A-3 and G-5 employment contracts contain all required elements and are electronically scanned for future reference in case of alleged abuse. State reiterated that it is primarily the responsibility of senior consular managers at posts to ensure compliance with visa adjudication procedures and practices in their consular sections, but added that it will consider and review whether spot-checking compliance from headquarters is appropriate and consistent with judicious use of limited resources. As indicated in our fourth recommendation, we believe that spot-checking is important for enhancing oversight and could be targeted in such a way as to minimize use of resources.

Justice generally agreed with our findings, particularly our finding that obstacles to investigating allegations of household worker abuse are compounded when employers have diplomatic immunity. Justice also concurred with our second recommendation, highlighting the importance of agreeing upon time frames for determining which investigative techniques can be used, so that criminal investigations are not compromised.

State, Justice, and Homeland Security provided technical comments, which we incorporated as appropriate. For example, Homeland Security asked to be included in the second recommendation, which was initially directed to the Secretary of State and the Attorney General. Specifically, Homeland Security officials stated that Immigration and Customs Enforcement should

participate in the recommended interagency process because the introduction of persons into the United States for the purpose of exploitation is a primary law enforcement responsibility and area of expertise of Immigration and Customs Enforcement. We agreed to include the Secretary of Homeland Security in the second recommendation.

The Departments of Labor and Health and Human Services did not provide comments on the draft report.

We are sending copies of this report to other interested Members of Congress. We are also sending copies to the Secretary of State, the Attorney General, the Secretary of Homeland Security, the Secretary of Labor, and the Secretary of Health and Human Services. In addition, the report will be available at no charge on the GAO Web site at http://www.gao.gov.

If you or your staffs have any questions about this report, please contact me at (202) 512-9601 or melitot@gao.gov. Contact points for our offices of Congressional Relations and Public Affairs may be found on the last page of this report. GAO staff who made significant contributions to this report are listed in appendix VI.

Thomas Melito
Director,
International Affairs and Trade

Appendix I: Objectives, Scope, and Methodology

Our objectives were to (1) seek to determine how many A-3 and G-5 visa holders have alleged abuse by foreign diplomats with immunity since 2000, (2) review the U.S. government's process for investigating abuse allegations involving foreign diplomats with immunity, and (3) describe and assess how State ensures correct and consistent implementation of A-3 and G-5 visa polices and procedures. In this report, we define abuse to include illegal activities ranging from wage and hour violations to human trafficking.

To determine how many A-3 and G-5 visa holders have alleged abuse by foreign diplomats from 2000 (when the U.S. government enacted the Trafficking Victims Protection Act) through June 2008, we collected data, interviewed officials from four U.S. government agencies and 10 nongovernmental organizations (NGO), and searched legal databases, such as Westlaw, to identify civil lawsuits.

- At the Department of State (State), we met with officials from the Office of the Legal Adviser, Office of the Chief of Protocol, Diplomatic Security Service, Office of Foreign Missions, Bureau of International Organizations Affairs, United States Mission to the United Nations (USUN), Office to Monitor and Combat Trafficking in Persons, and Bureau of African Affairs.
- At the Department of Justice (Justice), we met with officials from the Human Smuggling and Trafficking Prosecution Unit within the Civil Rights Division/Criminal Section (CRT/CS), Executive Office for United States Attorneys, headquarters and field offices of the Federal Bureau of Investigation (FBI), and one local Assistant United States Attorney's (AUSA) Office.
- At the Department of Homeland Security (Homeland Security), we met with officials from Immigration and Customs Enforcement's (ICE) Human Smuggling and Trafficking Unit and Citizenship and Immigration Services (CIS).
- At the Department of Labor (Labor) we met with officials from the Employment Standard Administration's Wage and Hour Division headquarters office and its New York City district office.
- We identified and met with 10 NGOs that have provided legal services to A-3 and G-5 visa holders through analysis of civil lawsuits filed on behalf of A-3 and G-5 visa holders, referrals from NGOs, and a review of past and recent media reports. These 10 NGOs have a broad range of experience and expertise on cases involving victims of household worker abuse and are all located in the Washington, D.C., and New York regions.

State, Justice, Homeland Security, and Labor provided data on the number of incidents they have handled by canvassing current staff and reviewing specific case files. To avoid double-counting the number of these alleged incidents, we asked the departments to verify with each other the number of investigations in which they had participated. Homeland Security also provided us with the number of individuals who had received T visas and identified themselves as A-3 or G-5 visa holders on their T visa applications. We counted NGO-alleged incidents if we could determine the name of the diplomat involved and confirm that he or she held immunity or if we received enough information from a law enforcement source to ensure that a diplomat with immunity was involved and that the alleged incident was not duplicative with any other incident. Therefore, we believe that the data we obtained from federal agencies and the NGOs are sufficiently reliable for reporting the minimum number of incidents of alleged abuse of A-3 and G-5 visa holders by their employers since 2000.

To review the U.S. government's process for investigating abuse allegations involving foreign diplomats with immunity, we reviewed State documents including the *Foreign Affairs Manual*, cables sent to consular officers on A-3 and G-5 visas, "Diplomatic and Consular Immunity Guidance for Law Enforcement and Judicial Authorities," diplomatic notes to Chiefs of Diplomatic Missions in the United States regarding conduct of diplomatic agents in the United States, USUN's diplomatic notes to Permanent Missions and Permanent Observer Offices, and State's 2007 document to the Senate Committee on Foreign Relations entitled "State's Initiatives to Promote Fair Treatment of Domestic Workers by Diplomatic Personnel." We also interviewed officials from State's Office of the Chief of Protocol, Office of the Legal Adviser, Diplomatic Security Service, USUN, and Office to Monitor and Combat Trafficking in Persons. Because federal law enforcement agencies have no written policies or procedures specifically regarding abuse of household workers by foreign diplomats, we relied on testimonial evidence to determine their processes for handling alleged abuse of household workers by foreign diplomats. We interviewed law enforcement officials from Justice including the FBI, the Human Smuggling and Trafficking Prosecution Unit within CRT/CS, and one AUSA Office. We also met with officials at the Human Smuggling and Trafficking Unit within ICE. We interviewed one of the two U.S. Attorneys assigned to prosecute two relevant cases. The second prosecutor did not comment about the case, given the early stage of the review. At Labor we reviewed a document describing the agency's policy regarding household workers employed by foreign nationals titled "Domestic Service Workers Employed by Foreign Nationals," and interviewed officials at the Wage and Hour Division headquarters office and the Office of Enforcement Policy and the New York City District Office. We also analyzed key sections of international conventions, acts, and agreements on immunity to describe in general terms the different levels of immunity and the protections accorded under each one, specifically with regard to investigations of alleged abuse or trafficking of household workers by foreign diplomats. Finally, we interviewed NGOs and three alleged victims of abuse by foreign diplomats.

To describe and assess how State ensures correct and consistent implementation of A-3 and G-5 visa polices and procedures, we reviewed documents, analyzed data provided to us by State, and interviewed State officials in Washington, D.C.; New York; Lima, Peru; Manila, Philippines; Doha, Qatar; and Riyadh, Saudi Arabia. We reviewed the *Foreign Affairs Manual*, State's circular notes, training and guidance materials for consular officers, and guidance for visa applicants on State's public Web site and consular posts' Web sites. We interviewed officials from State's headquarters, including Consular Affairs and the Office of the Chief of Protocol. We also interviewed consular officers and reviewed A-3 and G-5 applications at four consular posts: Lima, Peru; Manila, Philippines; Doha, Qatar; and Riyadh, Saudi Arabia. In selecting these four consular posts, we analyzed data provided to us by Consular Affairs on A-3 and G-5 visas issued for fiscal years 2000 through 2007. Each of the 4 posts is among the 10 that issued the most A-3 and G-5 visas, combined, during this time period. Together these four posts account for about 22 percent of all A-3 and G-5 visas issued abroad since 2000. The U.S. embassy in Manila issued more A-3 and G-5 visas from fiscal year 2000 through 2007 than any other overseas post. The total number of A-3 and G-5 visas issued in Manila accounts for almost 10 percent of all A-3 and G-5 visas issued during this period. The U.S. embassy in Lima issued the second highest number of A-3 and G-5 visas, about 5 percent of the total, and the U.S. embassies in Riyadh and Qatar followed closely behind Lima, with about 4 percent and 3 percent, respectively, of all A-3 and G-5 visas issued during this period.

As part of our site visits or through telephone interviews, we interviewed consular officers to determine the steps State's Bureau of Consular Affairs has taken to ensure that State's policies and procedures for issuing A-3 and G-5 visas are implemented correctly and consistently. To examine the procedures for issuing A-3 and G-5 visas, we reviewed documents describing the requirements that household workers and U.S. consular officers should meet during the visa application process. We did not review or evaluate consular officers' decisions to refuse or issue visas. We worked with State officials to identify documentation that we could review both at consular posts and in Washington, D.C.

To determine the extent to which A-3 and G-5 applications met documentation requirements, we developed a checklist of State's requirements for A-3 and G-5 visa applicants and then assessed applications at each post against this checklist, reconciling any differences in our assessments. For one of the four posts, we were able to review all available documentation for A-3 and G-5 visas adjudicated since March 1, 2007. (We selected this date because State issued updated guidance to posts on the A-3 and G-5 visa class in March 2007.) For the other three posts, we were able to review only a sample of available files and documentation. Although the cases we reviewed from these posts are not generalizable, we reviewed a randomly selected set of cases to minimize any selection bias. Below is a more detailed explanation of our methodology for selecting and reviewing files from each post:

- In Lima, Peru, we reviewed 87 A-3 and G-5 visa files that had been adjudicated between March 1, 2007, and February 26, 2008, and that had a paper copy of the employment contract, the diplomatic note, or both. While 53 additional A-3 and G-5 application files were not available for our review in Lima, Consular Affairs in Washington, D.C., later agreed to search the Consular Consolidated Database to determine whether any documents for these 53 files had been scanned into it. These officials also searched the database for scans of accompanying documents for any of the 87 files in Lima for which we had seen only one of the required documents. (For example, if we saw only a diplomatic note in a given file, we asked if the related employment contract had been scanned into the database.) The officials determined that documents that we had not reviewed, related to 2 of the 87 files in Lima, had been scanned into the database. They also determined that one or both of the required documents for 5 of the 53 files that were not available for review at post had been scanned into the database. We did not review these seven files.
- In Manila, Philippines, we reviewed 61 A-3 and G-5 visa application files from December 1, 2007, to March 15, 2008, including all available documentation. Due to physical space constraints, this post only maintains 3 months of visa applications on file. In addition, the post had not been scanning employment contracts or diplomatic notes into the Consular Consolidated Database, so we were unable to review any files earlier than December 2007.
- For Riyadh, Saudi Arabia, we reviewed a total of 25 A-3 or G-5 visa files. At post, we reviewed two application files, including all documentation available for these A-3 or G-5 visa applications. Although we had requested to review all files available since March 1, 2007, consular officials in Washington, D.C., instructed the post to allow us to review files only if the particular case was mentioned in the course of interviews at posts. These officials later agreed to

provide us redacted copies of 25 percent (or 23) of the A-3 and G-5 visa files from the U.S. Embassy in Riyadh between March 1, 2007 and February 29, 2008. We randomly selected these 23 files and reviewed them in Washington.

- In Doha, Qatar, we reviewed all 56 A-3 and G-5 visa application files that were adjudicated between March 1, 2007, and February 28, 2008, including all documentation available.

Although we were unable to review all requested A-3 and G-5 visa files at the posts we visited, the information we obtained was sufficient for addressing our third objective.

We conducted this performance audit between October 2007 and July 2008 in accordance with generally accepted government auditing standards. Those standards require that we plan and perform the audit to obtain sufficient, appropriate evidence to provide a reasonable basis for our findings and conclusions based on our audit objectives. We believe that the evidence obtained provides a reasonable basis for our findings and conclusions based on our audit objectives.

APPENDIX II: U.S. GOVERNMENT AGENCIES' PRIMARY RESPONSIBILITIES RELATED TO FOREIGN DIPLOMATS AND A-3 AND G-5 VISA HOLDERS

We also analyzed various federal agencies' role in investigating and prosecuting federal law violations related to abuse of household workers by foreign diplomats with some level of immunity. Table 2 summarizes our analysis.

We also analyzed various federal agencies' role in investigating and prosecuting federal law violations related to abuse of household workers by foreign diplomats with some level of immunity. Table 2 summarizes our analysis.

Table 1. Relevant Responsibilities of State Department Bureaus and Offices

Office	Responsibility
Office of the Chief of Protocol, Diplomatic Affairs Division	• Accredits diplomatic agents and consular officers of foreign governments in the United States • Maintains the official records regarding the status and immunity level of all diplomatic and consular officers • Makes available to the public the *Diplomatic List*and *Foreign Consular Offices in the United States* • Submits State's annual report to the Secretary of State and Congress entitled *Report on Criminal [and Civil] Cases Involving Immunity*
Bureau of Consular Affairs	• Issues policy, guidance, and training to consular officers on the adjudication of A-3and G-5 visas
U.S. Embassies and Consulates	• Adjudicates A-3and G-5 nonimmigrant visa applications (reviews documents and interviews visa applicant and, possibly, employer)
Office of the Legal Adviser, Consular Affairs	• Provides legal advice and representation in relation to the performance of consularfunctions by State (including adjudication and revocation of visas and passports)
Office of the Legal Adviser, Diplomatic Law and Litigation	• Advises law enforcement authorities on diplomatic and consular immunity
Office to Monitor and Combat Trafficking in Persons	• Encourages partnerships and leads the coordination of antitrafficking efforts both worldwide and domestically • Consults with nongovernmental organizations and affected victims of trafficking
United States Mission to the United Nations (USUN)	• Facilitates and evaluates registration and accreditation of individuals accredited by the United Nations • Communicates with the UN Protocol and Liaison Service for full listing in the publicly available *Blue Book*of the missions' diplomatic personnel and their spouses
Bureau of International Organizations	• Receives allegations of abuse by UN diplomats from USUN • Works in cooperation with the USUN and Office of the Legal Adviser, Diplomatic Law on allegations of abuse by UN diplomats

Source: GAO analysis of State documents and interviews.

Table 2. Federal Departments with Primary Investigative and Prosecutorial Responsibilities

Investigative and Prosecutorial Departments	Office	Responsibility
Justice	Civil Rights Division/Criminal Section, Human Trafficking Prosecution Unit	• Receives allegations that a crime has occurred • Refers cases to lead investigative agency, if the agency has not already begun an investigation • Prosecutes trafficking crimes in conjunction with the U.S. attorney for the relevant jurisdiction
	Federal Bureau of Investigation	• Investigates trafficking crimes
	U.S. Attorneys	• Prosecutes trafficking cases in their geographic jurisdiction in conjunction with the Human Trafficking Prosecution Unit
Homeland Security	Immigration and Customs Enforcement (ICE), Human Smuggling and Trafficking Unit	• Investigates human trafficking crimes and provides short-term immigration relief to alien victims (continued presence)
State	Bureau of Diplomatic Security Service, Criminal Investigation Division	• Investigates passport violations and visa fraud, which may be in connection with other serious crimes such as trafficking
Labor	Employment Standards Administration, Wage and Hour Division	• Maintains policy on wage and hour investigations involving foreign nationals attached to a foreign embassy, consulate, or internationalorganization • Notifies State of these investigations
Supporting Departments		
State	Office of the Legal Adviser, Diplomatic Law and Litigation	• Advises law enforcement authorities on diplomatic and consular immunity
	Office of the Chief of Protocol	• Refers alleged criminal violations to law enforcement authorities
Homeland Security	Citizenship and Immigration Services	• Processes and approves T nonimmigrant status for alien victims of trafficking • Processes short-term immigration relief for alien victims (continued presence)
Health and Human Services		• Oversees administration of benefits to T nonimmigrant status visa recipients

Source: GAO analysis of Justice, Homeland Security, State, Labor, and Health and Human Services documents and interviews.

APPENDIX III: DIPLOMATIC AND CONSULAR PRIVILEGES AND IMMUNITIES FROM CRIMINAL AND CIVIL JURISDICTION

Table 3. Diplomatic and Consular Privileges and Immunities from Criminal and Civil Jurisdiction

Category	May be arrested or detained	Residence may be entered subject to law enforcement procedures generally applicable to U.S. residences	May be prosecuted	Immunity from civil jurisdiction	Recognized family member
Diplomatic agent[a] (e.g., ambassadors and other diplomatic officers)	No[b]	No	No	Yes[c]	Same as sponsor (full immunity and inviolability).
Member of administrative and technical staff[c] (e.g., secretaries, certain clerical managers, office managers, and certain security personnel)	No[b]	No	No	Yes, for acts performed in the course of their official duties. Otherwise, no.	Same as sponsor. Since family members have no official duties to perform, they enjoy no immunity from civil jurisdiction.
Service staff[d] (e.g., drivers, cleaners, and building and maintenance workers)	Yes	Yes	No, for official acts. Otherwise yes.	Yes, for acts performed in course of their duties. Otherwise, no.	No immunity or inviolability.
Career consular officers[a,d]	No, except for a felony and pursuant to a warrant.	Yes[e]	No, for official acts. Otherwise, yes.	Yes, for acts performed in the exercise of consular functions.[f] Otherwise, no.	No immunity or inviolability.

Table 3. (Continued).

Honorary consular officers(e.g., American citizens or permanent resident aliens who perform consular services on a part-time basis.)	Yes	Yes	No, for official acts. Otherwise, yes.	Yes, for acts performed in the exercise of consular functions.[f] Otherwise, no.	No immunity or inviolability.
Category	May be arrested or detained	Residence may be entered subject to law enforcement procedures generally applicable to U.S. residences	May be prosecuted	Immunity from civil jurisdiction	Recognized family member
Consular employees[d] (e.g., those who perform the administrative and technical support services for the consular post)	Yes	Yes	No, for official acts. Otherwise, yes.	Yes, for acts performed in the exercise of consular functions.[f] Otherwise, no.	No immunity or inviolability.
International organizations staff[g]	Yes[g]	Yes[g]	No, for official acts. Otherwise, yes.[g]	Yes, for acts performed in the exercise of their official duties. Otherwise, no.[g]	No immunity or inviolability.[g]
Diplomatic-level staff of missions to international organizations	No[b]	No	No	Yes[c]	Same as sponsor (fullimmunity and inviolability).
Support staff of missions to international organizations	Yes	Yes	No, for official acts. Otherwise, yes.	Yes, for acts performed in the exercise of their official duties. Otherwise, no.	No immunity or inviolability.

Source: GAO.

[a] The Department of State, as a matter of policy, does not normally accept as bilateral diplomatic agents or as career consular officers U.S. nationals or legal permanent residents of the United States. Family members of diplomatic agents enjoy no privileges and immunities if they are U.S. nationals. Members of the administrative and technical staff (including their families) and members of the service staff enjoy no privileges and immunities if they are U.S. nationals, legal permanent residents, or foreign nationals permanently residing in the United States.

[b] Reasonable constraints, however, may be applied in emergency circumstances,e.g., self-defense, public safety, or the prevention of serious, violent criminal acts.

[c] Certain exceptions apply under Article 31 of the Vienna Convention on Diplomatic Relations. Immunity from civil and administrative jurisdiction does not apply in the following circumstances: (1) a real action relating to private immovable property situated in the territory of the receiving state unless the diplomatic agent holds it on behalf of the sending state for the purpose of the mission; (2) an action relating to succession in which the diplomatic agent is involved as executor, administrator, heir, or legatee as a private person and not on behalf of the sending state; (3) an action relating to any professional or commercial activity exercised by the diplomatic agent in the receiving state outside his official functions.

[d] This table presents general rules. Employees of certain foreign countries may enjoy higher levels of privileges and immunities on the basis of special bilateral agreements.

[e] Note that consular residences are sometimes located within the official consular premises. In such cases, only the official office space is protected from police entry unless a bilateral agreement provides additional protection for consular residences.

[f] This immunity does not apply in respect of a civil action either (1) arising out of a contract concluded by a consular officer or employee in which he did not contract expressly or impliedly as an agent of the sending state; or (2) by a third party for damage arising from an accident in the receiving state caused by a vehicle, vessel, or aircraft. See Article 43 of the Vienna Convention on Consular Relations.

[g] A small number of senior officers are entitled to be treated identically to “diplomatic agents.”

We analyzed key sections of international conventions, acts, and agreements on immunity to describe in general terms the different levels of immunity and the protections accorded under each one, specifically as they relate to investigations of alleged abuse of household workers by foreign diplomats. We also consulted with the Department of State on our analysis, which is summarized in table 3. This table represents only a general description of these privileges and immunities and, as indicated in the notes following the table, exceptions may apply for each general category.

APPENDIX IV: COMMENTS FROM THE DEPARTMENT OF STATE

United States Department of State

Assistant Secretary for Resource Management
and Chief Financial Officer

Washington, D.C. 20520

JUL 11 2008

Ms. Jacquelyn Williams-Bridgers
Managing Director
International Affairs and Trade
Government Accountability Office
441 G Street, N.W.
Washington, D.C. 20548-0001

Dear Ms. Williams-Bridgers:

We appreciate the opportunity to review your draft report, "HUMAN RIGHTS: U.S. Government's Efforts to Address Alleged Abuse of Household Workers by Foreign Diplomats with Immunity Could Be Strengthened," GAO Job Code 320533.

The enclosed Department of State comments are provided for incorporation with this letter as an appendix to the final report.

If you have any questions concerning this response, please contact Chenobia Calhoun, Office of Protocol at 202-647-1727, David Tyler, Bureau of Consular Affairs at 202-663-1155 and Susan Benda, Office of the Legal Adviser at 202-647-1074.

Sincerely,

B. Higgins

Bradford R. Higgins

cc: GAO – Al Huntington
S/OPR, CA/FO and L
State/OIG – Mark Duda

Department of State Comments on GAO Draft Report

HUMAN RIGHTS: U.S. Government's Efforts to Address Alleged Abuse of Household Workers by Foreign Diplomats with Immunity Could Be Strengthened (GAO-08-892, GAO Code 320533)

The Department of State appreciates the opportunity to comment on GAO's draft report entitled *"Human Rights: U.S. Government's Efforts to Address Alleged Abuse of Household Workers by Foreign Diplomats with Immunity Could Be Strengthened."*

The GAO report recommends the following to the Secretary of State:

Recommendation 1: To ensure that the Office of Protocol and the Office of the Legal Advisor are aware of all cases involving alleged abuse of household workers by foreign diplomats that have come to the attention of the department, we recommend that the Secretary of State (1) emphasize to the relevant bureaus and offices the importance of the Foreign Affairs Manual's requirement to report all cases that come to their attention and (2) direct the Office of Protocol and the Office of the Legal Advisor to create a system for collecting and maintaining records on these cases.

Response: The Department will emphasize to the relevant bureaus and offices the importance of reporting promptly and fully all cases of alleged abuse of household workers by foreign diplomats. The Office of Protocol is creating a system for collecting and maintaining centralized records on these cases that would allow for ready access to records of cases that involve individuals with immunity. The records would include the name of the employer and the employee, the nature of the allegation and the lever of immunity of the employer.

Recommendation 2: To assist in timely handling of future investigations, we recommend that the Secretary of State and the Attorney General establish an interagency process, outlining agreed upon policies, including timeframes, for determining which investigative techniques can be used in trafficking investigations involving foreign diplomats.

Response: The Department acknowledges that it would be useful to establish an agreed-upon interagency process to address trafficking and other investigations involving foreign diplomats, including a manner for timely communicating about the use of investigative techniques in these cases. While most investigations go forward without consultations on investigative techniques and, the Department generally answers promptly, the Department believes it will be useful to work with the Department of Justice to establish such a process to address novel and difficult questions regarding investigative techniques.

Recommendation 3: We recommend that the Secretary of State direct the Bureau of Consular Affairs, in coordination with the Office of Protocol and the Office of the Legal Adviser, to establish a system alerting consular officers to seek guidance from State headquarters before issuing A-3 or G-5 visas to applicants whose prospective employers may have abused their household workers in the past. For example, if State headquarters is aware that a foreign diplomat is under investigation for alleged human trafficking, it could place an alert in the system advising consular officers to request guidance should an individual apply for an A-3 or G-5 visa to work for that diplomat.

Response: The State Department's Bureau of Consular Affairs current visa name-check systems, including the Consular Lookout and Support System (CLASS) and Consular Consolidated Database (CCD), are designed to effectively screen applicants and maintain complete watch lists, and we will proactively watch-list known abusers in CLASS. With the deployment of the electronic visa application under the Consular Electronic Application Center (CEAC), the Visa Office will look for further opportunities to evaluate employers with the help of automation. The Department's Office of Foreign Missions (OFM) has a separate database system known as "The Office of Foreign Missions Information System" (TOMIS), which is used to track diplomats and international organization staff duly accredited in the United States. Currently, consular officers in the field and Washington have access to TOMIS. OFM will soon upgrade consular access to TOMIS to provide improved information regarding A-3 and G-5 cases, including sponsor's status in the United States. TOMIS provides an excellent vehicle for thorough checks of A-3 and G-5 visa applicants.

Recommendation 4: To better ensure correct and consistent implementation of A-3 and G-5 visa policies and procedures, particularly those that outline requirement for employment contracts, we recommend that the Secretary of State enhance oversight by establishing a system to spot-check compliance with these policies and procedures. This spot-check system would allow headquarters to assess compliance without dedicating the resources needed to review all A-3 and G-5 visas issued in a given year and could be targeted at posts that issue high numbers of A-3 or G-5 visas or that have identified difficulties interpreting guidance on these visa classes.

Response: We acknowledge the need for better compliance with policies and procedures to ensure that employment contracts contain all required elements and that all contracts are scanned into our system for future reference in case of alleged abuse. We are developing additional guidance on this issue for inclusion in the Foreign Affairs Manual (FAM), and as soon as this guidance is available for publication, we will remind posts of all requirements with regard to A-3 and G-5 visa adjudication. The amended FAM notes containing this guidance will also provide a clearer description of the circumstances establishing reason for a consular officer to believe that the employer is not in a position to pay the prevailing wage or may be otherwise abusing an employee such that the officer should refuse an A-3 or G-5visa to the employee.

Under current policies and controls, it is primarily the responsibility of senior consular managers at posts to ensure compliance with visa adjudication procedures and practices in their consular sections, and we will remind consular managers of the need to pay particular attention to A-3 and G-5 visa processes. As far as spot-checking from headquarters, the Bureau of Consular Affairs will take this under consideration and review whether such an approach is appropriate and consistent with judicious use of limited resources. As we move ahead towards an all-electronic visa application process, development of which is well underway, there will be greater opportunities to review and screen visa applications from our domestic operations facilities prior to the visa interview at post. This type of review is already occurring for temporary worker visas, and the concept may eventually be extended to reviewing other visa categories and prerequisite documents such as employment contracts. This approach promises to increase standardization and consistency worldwide for all types of visas, including the specific categories addressed in this report.

Appendix V: Comments from the Department of Justice

U.S. Department of Justice

Civil Rights Division

Office of the Assistant Attorney General

Washington, D.C. 20530

JUL 11 2008

Thomas Melito
Director, International Affairs and Trade
U.S. Government Accountability Office
441 G Street, N.W.
Washington, D.C. 20548

Dear Mr. Melito:

Thank you for the opportunity to review the final draft of the Government Accountability Office (GAO) report entitled "*HUMAN RIGHTS: U.S. Government's Efforts to Address Alleged Abuse of Household Workers by Foreign Diplomats with Immunity Could Be Strengthened, GAO*-08-892." This draft report was reviewed by the Department of Justice's components that participated in the review. This letter constitutes the Department's formal comments. I request that the GAO include this letter in the final report. The Department's technical comments were provided under separate cover.

The report defines "alleged abuse" of household workers broadly, to include not only allegations of human trafficking, but also allegations of wage and hour violations and other misconduct. The Department of Justice takes allegations of human trafficking very seriously, and these prosecutions are a priority of the Department. In the last seven fiscal years, the Civil Rights Division, in conjunction with the U.S. Attorneys' Offices, has increased by nearly seven-fold the number of human trafficking cases filed in court as compared to the previous seven fiscal years. In FY 2007, the Department obtained a record number of convictions in human trafficking prosecutions. Since 2005, the Department has investigated 19 alleged cases of human trafficking by persons with diplomatic immunity, with many of these cases involving multiple subjects and victims. Many of these investigations are ongoing, and one of these investigations has resulted in the Department of Justice notifying the Department of State that, but for the subject's immunity, the Department of Justice would seek an indictment of the subject.

As this report notes, human trafficking investigations and prosecutions are very complex in general, and investigations of forced household labor are particularly challenging because the victims are isolated in private homes, are fearful of retaliation in their home country, and are often members of vulnerable populations who are unfamiliar with our legal system or the rights and services available to them. As the report finds, these obstacles to investigating allegations of

Mr. Thomas Melito Page Two

forced household labor are compounded when subjects have diplomatic immunity, which impacts our ability to conduct certain valuable investigative techniques that, in other cases, have served to corroborate allegations of forced labor. Nevertheless, the Department of Justice is committed to conducting complete and thorough investigations of all allegations.

Recommendation that the Attorney General and the Secretary of State Establish an Interagency Process Outlining Agreed Upon Policies, Including Timeframes, For Determining Which Investigative Techniques Can Be Used In Trafficking Investigations Involving Foreign Diplomats

The Department of Justice does not object to this recommendation. As the report notes, the Department of Justice and the Department of State are already engaging in regular collaborative meetings in an effort to address the impact of diplomatic immunity on human trafficking investigations on a case-by-case basis. Further meetings should assist both Departments in understanding the legal framework for analyzing the impact of diplomatic immunity on certain investigative techniques and improve our ability to expediently determine which investigative techniques are legally permissible. The Department of Justice also supports the report's recommendation that any agreed upon policies for resolving these issues include timeframes that ensure deliberations and decisions on these investigative issues are resolved expediently so as not to compromise the criminal investigation.

The Department of Justice notes, however, that despite the significant increase in the trafficking caseload since 2001 using existing resources, additional resources are needed if we are to continue our successful investigation and prosecution of human trafficking crimes and to further our collaborative efforts with the Department of State and our other partners.

The extensive effort that your staff has put into this report and the opportunity to work with them on this important issue are appreciated.

Sincerely,

Grace Chung Becker
Acting Assistant Attorney General

cc: Ms. Cheryl Goodman
Assistant Director, International Affairs and Trade
U.S. Government Accountability Office

End Notes

[1] For the purposes of this report, the term "foreign diplomats" is defined to include members of diplomatic missions (diplomatic agents, administrative and technical staff, and service staff), individuals assigned to consular posts (consular officers, consular employees, and

honorary consuls), and employees of international organizations or members of national missions to such international organizations.

[2] Under the Trafficking Victims Protection Act, victims of severe forms of trafficking are defined, in part, as persons subject to the recruitment, harboring, transportation, provision, or obtaining of persons for labor or services, through the use of force, fraud, or coercion, for the purpose of subjection to involuntary servitude, peonage, debt bondage, or slavery. Congress enacted the Trafficking Victims Protection Act (Public L. No. 106-386) in 2000 and reauthorized and amended this act in 2003 and again in 2005 (Public L. Nos. 108-193 and 109-164).

[3] Foreign diplomats may be entitled to some degree of immunity (full or partial) or may have no immunity at all. Foreign diplomats' property also may be inviolable, meaning that it cannot be entered or searched without the diplomats' consent. See app. III for more information on the respective privileges and immunities to which various categories of foreign diplomats are entitled.

[4] In 2006, the woman's lawyers filed a new lawsuit on her behalf, arguing that because the diplomat and his wife have left the United States, they no longer hold criminal and civil immunity for activities unrelated to their official acts. That litigation is pending.

[5] Foreign officials for international organizations may be employees of these organizations or members of diplomatic missions to the organizations. In addition, if a foreign diplomat is traveling to the United States on unofficial business, his or her household workers may receive B-1 visas.

[6] The *Foreign Affairs Manual* is a State publication that outlines guidance and requirements for State Department employees.

[7] The federal minimum wage was recently increased to $6.55 per hour. Many states also have minimum wage laws. In cases where an employee is subject to both the state and federal minimum wage laws, the employee is entitled to the higher of the two minimum wages. The prevailing wage rate is defined as the average wage paid to similarly employed workers in the requested occupation in the area of intended employment.

[8] An employer must be entitled to an A-1 or A-2 nonimmigrant visa classification in order to bring individuals under A-3 visa status to the United States to work in his or her home. An employer must be entitled to a G-1, G-2, G-3, or G-4 nonimmigrant visa classification in order to bring individuals under G-5 visa status to the United States to work in his or her home. (See Immigration and Nationality Act, as amended, §101(a)(15)(A)(iii) and §101(a)(15)(G)(v)). As a matter of policy, A-3 and G-5 visas are issued for a maximum period of 24 months, or less, if called for by the reciprocity schedule of the country concerned. In addition, the validity of an A-3 or G-5 visa may not exceed the validity of the employer's visa.

[9] The number of A-3 visa applications also declined during this period. State officials told us they could not attribute any policy changes, procedural reasons, or particular events to the decline in A-3 visa issuances.

[10] Continued presence is granted to trafficking victims in accordance with Section 107(c)(3) of the Trafficking Victims Protection Act. Pursuant to 28 C.F.R. Part 1100.35, Homeland Security has the authority to grant continued presence to victims of severe forms of trafficking who are potential witnesses to such trafficking in order to ensure prosecution of those responsible.

[11] T nonimmigrant status is granted for victims of trafficking under INA Sec. 101(a)(15)(T). To qualify for a T visa, a victim must be present in the United States, American Samoa, or the Commonwealth of the Northern Mariana Islands as a result of trafficking. The individual

also must be a victim of a severe form of trafficking who would suffer extreme hardship upon removal and has complied with any reasonable request for assistance in the investigation and prosecution of human trafficking. The victim does not need to comply with requests for assistance in investigations and prosecutions if he or she is less than 18 years old.

[12] The United States has entered into a number of treaties that afford immunities. These treaties include the Vienna Convention on Consular Relations, 21 U.S.T 77, T.I.A.S., 6820, the Vienna Convention on Diplomatic Relations, 23 U.S.T. 3227, T.I.A.S. 7502, and the Agreement between the United Nations and the United States of America Regarding the Headquarters of the United Nations, 21 U.S.T. 1418, as well as bilateral agreements with certain countries. The U.S. Congress also enacted legislation, the International Organizations Immunities Act (22 U.S.C. §§ 288 et seq.), to extend certain privileges, exemptions, and immunities to international organizations and their employees.

[13] State's Office of Protocol makes available the following online publications: *Diplomatic List* (http://www.state which lists members of the diplomatic staff who have diplomatic rank and their spouses, and *Foreign Consular Offices* (http://www.state.gov/s/cpr/rls/fco/), which lists recognized consular officers in the United States. The United Nations publishes lists of diplomatic members and their spouses through an online publication known as the *Blue Book* (http://missions

[14] 32.5 percent of these foreign diplomats came from Africa, 30 percent from the Near East, 20 percent from the Western Hemisphere, 15 percent from Asia, and 2.5 percent from Europe.

[15] We only counted cases if we could determine the name of the diplomat involved and confirm that he or she held immunity, or if we received enough information from a law enforcement source to ensure that a diplomat with immunity was involved and that the case was not duplicative with any other case. Because GAO is not a law enforcement agency, we did not independently assess the credibility of these alleged incidents.

[16] Some allegations may be handled by both the U.S. government and an NGO. To avoid double counting the total number of allegations, we report each allegation under only one source. For example, if the U.S. government opened an investigation after receiving an allegation from an NGO, we included the case in our count of allegations handled by federal agencies, rather than in our count of allegations handled by NGOs.

[17] Each alleged incident may involve several instances of alleged abuse. For example, one alleged incident may involve different forms of abuse (such as verbal and physical abuse), as well as multiple instances of the same type of abuse.

[18] One of these investigations was opened in response to three separate allegations against the same foreign diplomat. In addition, civil suits were filed in three of these eight investigations. Justice officials told us that they have opened 19 trafficking investigations involving foreign diplomats with immunity since 2005. We confirmed that 8 of them were included in our count of 42 distinct alleged incidents.

[19] In this incident, a foreign diplomat brought an individual to the United States on an A-3 visa and then transferred her to his relatives, who allegedly abused her.

[20] In one of these cases, the judgment was later reversed on appeal, when the appellate court, in part, determined that the diplomat's employment of a household worker was not an act performed in the exercise of his consular functions and therefore he was not entitled to claim immunity under the Vienna Convention on Consular Relations.

[21] GAO, *Human Trafficking: Better Data, Strategy, and Reporting Needed to Enhance U.S. Antitrafficking Efforts Abroad*, GAO-06-825 (Washington, D.C.: July 18, 2006). See also GAO, *Human Trafficking: Monitoring and Evaluation of International Projects Are*

Limited, but Experts Suggest Improvements, GAO-07-1034 (Washington, D.C.: July 26, 2007).

[22] GAO, *Human Trafficking: A Strategic Framework Could Help Enhance the Interagency Collaboration Needed to Effectively Combat Trafficking Crimes*, GAO-07-915 (Washington, D.C.: July 26, 2007).

[23] Justice officials routinely report human trafficking investigations involving foreign diplomats to State's Office of the Legal Adviser. According to an official with the Office of the Legal Adviser, these reports are passed on to the Office of Protocol.

[24] We do not identify these techniques in this report because Justice and Homeland Security consider this information to be law-enforcement sensitive.

[25] We requested to review all employment contracts submitted by A-3 and G-5 visa applicants since March 2007 at the four consular posts we visited. We chose this date because State issued updated guidance to posts on A-3 and G-5 visas at that time. However, for reasons outlined in app. I, we were unable to review all relevant contracts at three of the four posts. For these three posts, we reviewed a random sample of cases to minimize any biases in selection of cases for review. We reviewed 45 contracts at the first post, 20 at the second, 57 at the third, and 16 at the fourth.

[26] This post has created a template employment contract for A-3 and G-5 visa applicants that meets State's requirements and is available on its Web site.

[27] It is possible that a contract in a language familiar to the applicant was presented at the interview, but was not maintained on file at the consular post. However, consular officers at this post did not express familiarity with the requirement that A-3 and G-5 visa applicants present contracts in a language that they understand and one officer told us that A-3 and G-5 contracts are always in English.

[28] The guidance refers consular officers to the trafficking hotline operated by the Department of Health and Human Services—1 (888) 373-7888. Justice also operates a trafficking hotline, which some NGOs have called on behalf of foreign diplomats' household workers. This toll-free hotline is 1 (888) 428-7581.

[29] One of the handouts directs applicants to the "Be Smart, Be Safe" brochure on State's Web site. However, neither of the handouts is as thorough as State's brochure in explaining what trafficking is, how to avoid becoming a trafficking victim, and how to get help if needed.

[30] According to State officials, accessing a copy of the contract is also useful because its scanned image may provide criminal investigators with evidence of visa fraud, as the issuance of the relevant A-3 or G-5 visa was based on the contract.

[31] Consular officials in Washington told us that instituting this type of policy is not appropriate.

[32] Although State has instituted Consular Management Assessment Teams to review select consular posts for, among other things, training and knowledge of consular functions, supervisory reviews of daily adjudications, and other visa issues, these teams are focused primarily on preventing visa malfeasance and are, therefore, unlikely to assess posts' compliance with A-3 and G-5 visa policies and procedures.

INDEX

A

B

C

J

L

M

N

O

P

R

S

T

U

V

W

Designing Care That Works

A Step-by-Step Guide to Building Programs that Heal

By

Mardoche Sidor, MD;
Karen Dubin, PhD, LCSW;
and the SWEET Institute

Transformational Books for a Transformational World

Acclaims for Designing Care That Works

Lydia Watling, LMSW (Children and Families)

"Designing Care That Works is the book I have been waiting for my entire career. It translates compassion into structure and gives those of us working with children and families a clear, actionable way to build programs that truly support growth, healing, and connection."

Carie Micelli, LMSW (Criminal Justice System)

"A masterclass in designing systems that stand with people where they are, even in the most complex and high-stakes environments. Essential reading for anyone working in justice-involved care."

Jenna Tine, LCSW (Senior Leadership)

"This book does what most leadership training fails to do. It shows you exactly how to build something that works, sustains, and scales. A blueprint for real-world leadership."

Alison Dockery, PhD (Psychology, Burnout, and Criminal Justice)

"Bold, practical, and deeply needed. This book takes the conversation beyond burnout and into transformation of individuals, teams, and entire systems."

Robert Nussbaum, PhD (Private Practice)

"An extraordinary synthesis of clinical insight and systems thinking. This book elevates how we understand care itself."

Adaiah Lasalle, LCSW (Internalized oppression)

"Transformational. This book doesn't just help you understand systems. It gives you the power to rewrite them."

Anne-Elizabeth Straub, LCSW-R (Advocacy)

"A call to action for the entire profession. This is how social work moves from intention to impact."

Adolfo Marero, LCSW (Administration)

"Finally, clarity. This book demystifies program design and gives administrators a real path forward."

Deirdre Powell (Doctoral Candidate)

"This is the book I wish every doctoral student had on day one. It's rigorous, relevant, and immediately applicable. Frameworks are essential to the design and implementation of every healing method. The authors clearly create a path for clinicians to be the healing they expect to see!"

Stuart Aaronson, LCSW-R (Hospital Administration & Education)

"An explicit roadmap. A landmark contribution. Will inspire hope in every provider in every helping system."

Emmanuel Charles, DSW (Hospital Administrator)

"Operational brilliance meets human-centered care. This is how systems should be built."

Vilma Gordon, LCSW-R (Clinic Administration)

"A practical guide to building programs that actually deliver results, without losing the human touch."

Donna Sue Johnson, LCSW-R (LGBTQI+ Advocacy)

"This book honors identity, dignity, and lived experience while showing us how to build systems that truly include everyone."

Irit Maor, LCSW (Private Practice)

"A rare and powerful bridge between clinical insight and real-world implementation. This book doesn't just describe what's wrong—it shows exactly how to build what works."

Lynwana Johnson, LMSW (Writer)

"This powerful work challenges clinicians to rethink how they engage, assess, and care plan by dismantling fragmented models that fail under the weight of their own disconnect. Instead, it champions transformative system designs that empower clinicians to bridge service gaps and build intentional programs that prioritize a healing-centered approach. This book doesn't just inform. It moves you!"

Marsha Redd, LMSW (Family & Couple Therapy)

"A transformative lens for understanding relationships, not just between people, but within systems."

Yokasta Lopez-Irving, LCSW (School & Geriatric Work)

"From classrooms to elder care, this book offers a universal framework for designing care across the lifespan."

Jose Vasquez, LCSW (Group Practice)

"A game changer for clinicians building practices and programs. Clear, structured, and immediately usable."

Monique Anderson, LMSW, RN (Managed Care)

"This book bridges clinical care and system design in a way that managed care has long needed."

Annette Jarrett-Graham, DNP (The Psychiatric NP's Handbook)

"An essential resource for psychiatric nurse practitioners and advanced clinicians alike. Practical, insightful, and highly relevant to modern mental health care."

Wendy Yewande Mikoku, NP

"A powerful integration of community psychiatry and practical program design. This book belongs in every clinical setting."

Lemaire Pierre, MD

"A visionary work. This is how we move psychiatry forward: from isolated care to integrated systems."

Philipe Douyon, MD

"Brilliant. This book aligns brain, behavior, and systems into one coherent model of transformation."

Jay Korman, LCSW

"This is leadership in action. A defining text for organized social work and beyond."

Karen Sumpter, LMSW

"A roadmap for leaders ready to build, not just manage. Clear, actionable, and deeply inspiring."

Ruth Smith, LCSW-R

"Finally, a book that connects program development with real-world application. A gift to the field."

Clovis Raymond, MD (Leadership)

"Grounded in both science and lived experience, this work redefines how we think about engagement, equity, and system design. A must-read for modern mental health and social service leaders."

Doreen Plante, LCSW

"Grounded, practical, and deeply human. This book will change how clinicians approach their work."

Jules Ranz, MD

"A critically important contribution to community psychiatry. This book addresses a gap in our field that has existed for decades."

Jacob Appel, MD

"An intellectually rigorous and ethically grounded guide to program design. This book reframes systems as moral structures, and shows us how to build them better."

Published by:

SWEET Institute Publishing
New York, NY
www.sweetinstitutepublishing.com

First Edition
Printed in the United States of America

ISBN (Paperback): 978-1-968105-46-4
ISBN (Hardcover): 978-1-968105-47-1
ISBN (eBook): 978-1-968105-48-8
Library of Congress Control Number: 2026941460

Cover Design by SWEET Institute Publishing
Interior Design and Layout by SWEET Institute Publishing

For bulk orders, permissions, or media inquiries, please contact:
sweetinstitutepublishing@sweetinstitute.com

Unless otherwise noted, all stories and case examples in this book are either fictionalized or used with permission. Identifying details have been changed to protect the privacy of individuals.

SWEET Institute Publishing
Transformational Books for a Transformational World

SWEET Institute Publishing — Universal Disclaimer

In Memory of Frederick Shack, LMSW

Leader, mentor, advocate, and visionary.

His belief in the dignity, depth, and potential of every human being continues to shape the work that follows.

Dedication

To everyone who has ever stood in the gap—
between what is and what could be.

To the clinicians who kept showing up, long after the system stopped trying.
To the leaders who chose courage, when comfort would've been easier.
To the social workers, case managers, outreach workers, nurses, physicians,
and quiet warriors who refused to let despair have the last word.

To every resident, client, patient, student, parent, elder, or neighbor
who ever felt unseen, unheard, or underserved—
this book is an act of recognition: You were never the problem. You were the reason.

To the next generation of changemakers: may you build systems worthy of the people who depend on them.

And to the ones who whispered
"there has to be a better way"… you were right.
This book is for you, all of you: the ones who never stopped believing
that healing is possible, not by accident, but by design.

Other Titles from SWEET Institute Publishing

- Always Enough: The Transformational Power of Unconditional Positive Regard: How to See, Accept, and Elevate Yourself and Others Through the 4 Layers of Transformation
- Because of Us: Why Outcomes Change When We Do
- Before Anything Else, Validate: The Missing Link in Healing, Leadership, Relationships, and Personal Growth
- One Habit at a Time: The Art and Science of Sustainable Change
- Rewriting the Script: The Power of Transforming Inner Dialogue in Oppressed Communities
- The Clinician's Mirror: A Story of Projection, Self-Awareness, and Transformation for Clinicians
- The Courage to Care: Stories of Healing, Hope, and the Power of Social Work — Told by Over 50 SWEET Institute Social Workers
- The Psychiatric Nurse Practitioner's Handbook: Healing with Precision, Presence, and Power

Acknowledgments

Every book is a collaboration, but this one carries the fingerprints of an entire ecosystem: people, teams, communities, mentors, and visionaries whose belief in human possibility makes the work of designing care both necessary and urgent.

We begin by expressing our deepest gratitude to the individuals and families whose lives and stories are reflected across every page. You are the reason we do this work. Your courage, persistence, vulnerability, and resilience have taught us more than any textbook ever could. This book honors you.

To the clinicians, case managers, social workers, psychiatrists, nurses, peer specialists, counselors, and direct-care staff across the country, especially those serving in community mental health, supportive housing, schools, shelters, hospitals, street outreach, and reentry programs: thank you. You show up every day with heart, skill, and determination, often under conditions that would overwhelm anyone else. You are the backbone of every effective program, and this book is written for you.

To the leaders and administrators who hold systems together, balancing vision and reality, compassion and compliance, innovation and regulation: your work is both invisible and indispensable. We see you; we honor you; and we hope this book strengthens the systems you steward.

We extend profound appreciation to Urban Pathways for modeling innovation, compassion, and visionary leadership in serving populations with high acuity needs. To Frederick Shack, LMSW, for his unwavering commitment to dignity, equity, and systemic transformation: your leadership has shaped this book more than words can express.

To the Columbia University Public & Community Psychiatry Fellowship, and to Dr. Stephanie LeMelle, MD, and Dr. Jules Ranz, MD, whose leadership, mentorship, and scholarship continue to elevate the field of community psychiatry. Your vision for training the next generation of leaders has influenced every idea in these pages.

To the dozens of directors, supervisors, and program managers who generously invited us into their programs: thank you for your wisdom, honesty, and collaboration. Your questions, frustrations, breakthroughs, and innovations helped shape a blueprint that is both practical and deeply human.

We extend our sincere gratitude to Jacob M. Appel, MD, JD, MPH, MPhil, for his thoughtful contribution to this work and for his enduring leadership at the intersection of psychiatry, ethics, and medical education. As an emergency room psychiatrist and a leading voice in bioethics, Dr. Appel brings a rare depth of insight into how systems shape care, and how ethical principles must be translated into real-world practice. His perspective has helped sharpen the vision of this book, grounding it in both intellectual rigor and practical relevance. We are honored to have his voice as part of this work.

To the entire SWEET Institute community: our members, learners, instructors, and collaborators, thank you for your trust, your brilliance, and your belief in a world transformed through presence, clarity, and intentional practice. You have proven, again and again, that learning can be a catalyst for action, and action a catalyst for transformation.

To our families, who have supported us, grounded us, encouraged us, and given us the time, space, and love required for work like this: thank you. Your presence makes everything possible.

We would also like to extend our deepest gratitude to the educators, mentors, and leaders who have shaped generations of clinicians and, in turn, influenced the vision behind this book. We thank Charmaine Rapaport, MD, former Training Director in General Psychiatry at New York Medical College; Cynthia Telingator, MD, and Sandra DeJong, MD, former Training Directors in Child and Adolescent Psychiatry at Cambridge Health Alliance, Harvard Medical School; James Knoll, MD, Training Director in Forensic Psychiatry at SUNY Upstate Medical University; Leo Bernhardt, MD, and Guillermo Santiago, MD, former attending physicians at New York Medical College, Metropolitan Hospital; Charles Perkel, MD, former Training Director of Addiction Psychiatry at Mount Sinai Beth Israel; Melinda Lantz, MD, former Vice Chair for Medical Education and former Training Director of Geriatric Psychiatry at Mount Sinai Beth Israel; and Lea Marin, MD, Training Director of the Geriatric Psychiatry Fellowship at Mount Sinai Beth Israel; and Annelle Primm, MD, former Deputy Medical Director of the American Psychiatric Association, whose national leadership in advancing culturally responsive and equitable mental health care continues to shape the field. Your commitment to excellence in training, mentorship, and patient care has left an enduring impact on the field and on all who have had the privilege to learn from you.

We are equally grateful to the leadership of the Black Psychiatrists of America, whose work continues to advance equity, representation, and excellence in mental health care, and to the American Psychiatric Association (APA) SAMHSA Fellowship Program, a transformative initiative that has shaped the careers of countless clinicians dedicated to serving underserved communities. We offer special recognition in honor of the late Marilyn King, whose leadership as Coordinator of the SAMHSA Fellowship Program created opportunities, opened doors, and inspired generations of fellows. To all the fellows of the APA SAMHSA Fellowship Programs, past and present, your commitment to service, leadership, and systemic change continues to move the field forward.

And finally, to every reader holding this book: Thank you for caring enough to build something better. Thank you for believing that systems can change. Thank you for stepping into the role of designer, leader, healer, and transformer.

May this book serve you well. May it strengthen your work. May it help you design care that truly works for individuals, families, teams, and communities.

With gratitude,
Mardoche Sidor, MD
Karen Dubin, PhD, LCSW
The SWEET Institute

Prologue

The Space Between Systems

It was supposed to be a routine visit: just a check-in, or a follow-up, or just another name on a long list. When they opened the door, he was sitting on the edge of the bed. He was still. He was not agitated, and he was not asking for anything. He was just… there. He hadn't eaten in days. His medications hadn't been taken in weeks; and on the table were discharge papers from two different hospitals, three days apart.

"Did anyone come by?" someone asked.

He shrugged. *"They told me to follow up."*

"With who?"

Another shrug.

On paper, he had everything: a psychiatrist, a case manager, a primary care provider, a benefits coordinator, and a housing program. Yet, in reality, he had no one. Each system had done its part, but nothing had been done, for no one had asked the most important question: Who is responsible for the whole person?

Later that day, the conversation began: *"What happened?"*

"He didn't follow up." "He didn't engage." "He missed appointments." However, something felt incomplete; and so, someone asked a different question: What did the system fail to do?

The answer was not in one place. It was in the space between them. It was between the hospital and the community; and between the referral and the follow-up; and between intention and experience; and that space is where people fall; and they do not fall because they are unwilling; rather, they fall because no one designed the space between.

In other words, we do not have a shortage of services. We have a shortage of systems that work; and this book was written because caring is not enough. It was written for the clinician, the leader, the team who know something is missing; and what is missing is not effort; rather, it is design.

Every system is perfectly designed to produce the results it currently produces. If people are falling through the cracks, then the cracks are part of the design; and this book is about closing those cracks by building differently, and by designing programs that connect, align, adapt, and sustain, for the goal is not to do more. The goal is to build something that works, for people don't fall through the cracks. They fall between systems that were never designed to meet; and that is what this book is here to change.

Table of Contents

Foreword

by Frederick Shack, LMSW

Emeritus Chief Executive Officer, Urban Pathways
Adjunct Faculty, Columbia University School of Social Work
Board Member
In honor of his life, leadership, and enduring legacy.

For more than three decades, I have worked at the intersection of homelessness, behavioral health, poverty, trauma, and the social determinants that shape every aspect of human possibility. I have witnessed systems rise to meet the needs of the moment, and I have watched those same systems fall short, and sometimes despite the very best intentions.

Across that span of time, one truth has become unmistakably clear: Programs alone do not change lives. People do. And systems either empower those people or get in their way.

Designing Care That Works arrives at a critical moment for our field. The challenges faced by the individuals and communities we serve are more complex, more interconnected, and more urgent than ever. Clinicians, front-line staff, program directors, and leaders are being asked to solve problems that no single discipline, agency, or sector can address alone. What the authors, and the SWEET Institute have created here is more than a manual. It is a blueprint: one built on the belief that care must be intentionally designed, thoughtfully implemented, and continuously strengthened. This book offers what our sector has needed for years. It offers clarity in a world of fragmented services. It helps provide structure for professionals who are too often told to "figure it out;" and it gives a shared language that clinicians, administrators, funders, and policymakers can use together. It also provides a pathway from idea to program, to system and to ecosystem. Lastly, it provides a human-centered, equity-driven framework that honors the dignity of every person we serve.

Through a blend of storytelling, science, practical tools, and visionary thinking, this book helps us do what we need to continue to do more: build programs that are coherent, compassionate, sustainable, and effective.

At Urban Pathways, we know what is at stake. Our residents deserve care that sees the whole person. Our staff deserve systems that support and not overwhelm them; and our city deserves solutions that rise to the sophistication of the challenges before us.

This book helps remind everyone what it takes. More importantly, it reminds us of something even deeper: that we are capable of building systems grounded in validation, equity, humanity, and hope—systems worthy of the people who rely on them.

Whether you are a clinician beginning your journey, an experienced leader navigating complexity, a policymaker shaping the future, or a partner committed to collective impact, I believe this book will become an essential companion in your work. It is practical, rigorous, visionary, and it is long overdue.

I am proud to stand beside the authors in this mission, and proud to offer this foreword for a book that I believe will transform not only programs, but lives, for when we design care that truly works, we do more than meet needs; we expand possibilities.

Frederick Shack, LMSW
Emeritus Chief Executive Officer, Urban Pathways
Adjunct Faculty, Columbia University School of Social Work
Board Member

Preface

by Jules Ranz, MD

Former Director, Columbia Public & Community Psychiatry Fellowship
Professor of Clinical Psychiatry, Columbia University Vagelos College of Physicians and Surgeons

For most of my career, I have worked alongside clinicians, program directors, and leaders who care deeply about the individuals they serve: people living with serious mental illness, trauma histories, poverty, homelessness, substance use, and the social conditions that too often determine both suffering and survival.

What has always struck me is not a lack of passion, expertise, or commitment. It is the absence of a clear framework: a roadmap for how to design, implement, evaluate, and sustain programs that genuinely meet the needs of the people we aim to help.

We train clinicians extraordinarily well in diagnosis, psychotherapy, and psychopharmacology. We train leaders in administration, budgeting, and systems navigation. However, we rarely teach anyone how to design a program that works. This gap has consequences: duplicated services, fragmented care, inconsistent implementation, overwhelmed clinicians, and most importantly, individuals and families who fall through the cracks. That is why Designing Care That Works is so urgently needed.

The authors and the SWEET Institute have created something that our field has been missing for decades: a step-by-step, accessible, deeply human guide that bridges the space between clinical knowledge and real-world systems of care. It is a rare achievement to write a book that is: practical, offering tools that clinicians can use tomorrow; scientific, integrating the evidence and theory behind effective program design; visionary, showing what is possible when systems align; and deeply compassionate, honoring both clients and the workforce that serves them. The storytelling is vivid, the conversations are authentic, and the frameworks, rooted in the SWEET 4-Layer Model, provide a way of thinking that is both intuitive and transformational.

What I appreciate most is that this book does not assume that change will come from policy shifts alone, or from heroic individual clinicians. It invites us to understand that lasting change arises from deliberate design, from programs built with clarity, equity, collaboration, and humanity at their core.

For those working with populations with high-acuity needs, who deserve far more than the fragmented systems they often encounter, this book provides a path forward. It is for clinicians seeking grounding and structure; for leaders seeking coherence and sustainability; and for systems seeking integration and impact. It offers exactly the kind of guidance our field has been waiting for.

As such, it is my hope that Designing Care That Works becomes required reading for every clinician, administrator, and policymaker committed to improving the well-being of individuals and communities, for when we design better programs, we create better systems; and when we create better systems, we make recovery and dignity possible for everyone.

Jules Ranz, MD
Former Director, Columbia Public & Community Psychiatry Fellowship
Professor of Clinical Psychiatry
Columbia University Vagelos College of Physicians and Surgeons

Introduction

by Jacob M. Appel, MD, JD, MPH, MPhil

Professor of Psychiatry and Medical Education, Icahn School of Medicine at Mount Sinai
Director of Ethics Education in Psychiatry, Icahn School of Medicine at Mount Sinai
Assistant Director, Academy for Medicine & the Humanities
Emergency Room Psychiatrist, Mount Sinai Health System

In the emergency department, time compresses. Decisions that might otherwise unfold over weeks, such as care plans, ethical deliberations, system coordination, must occur in minutes. A patient arrives in crisis: disoriented, distressed, often carrying not only symptoms, but the accumulated weight of trauma, instability, and systemic fragmentation. In these moments, clinicians are asked to do something extraordinary: to deliver care that is clinically sound, ethically grounded, and systemically effective, often within structures that were not designed to support such precision.

This is where a difficult truth emerges. The quality of care is not determined solely by the skill of the clinician, but by the design of the system in which that clinician operates. In this vein, there is an ethical problem hidden in plain sight. In bioethics, we are trained to think in terms of principles: autonomy, beneficence, nonmaleficence, justice. Yet in practice, these principles do not operate in isolation. They are mediated, sometimes constrained, by the systems through which care is delivered. A clinician may wish to act beneficently, but lack the resources to do so. A team may strive for justice, but operate within structures that produce inequitable outcomes. A program may be built with the intention of reducing harm, yet inadvertently perpetuate fragmentation, duplication, or exclusion. What appears, on the surface, to be a clinical failure is often, at its core, a design failure; and design failures are ethical failures.

Despite the centrality of systems in shaping outcomes, we do not systematically train clinicians in program design. We teach diagnosis, treatment, documentation, risk assessment, and crisis management. However, we do not teach, with the same rigor, how to build a program, how to structure a system of care, how to align services across sectors, how to design for sustainability, and how to ensure that ethical intentions translate into real-world outcomes. As a result, clinicians are often left to navigate systems they did not design, attempting to repair gaps they did not create, within constraints they cannot easily change. This is neither efficient nor ethical.

Designing Care That Works addresses this gap with clarity and ambition. Drs. Sidor, Dubin, and the SWEET Institute have developed a framework that is both practical and philosophically grounded, and one that recognizes that effective care requires alignment across multiple dimensions, including individual engagement, team functioning, organizational structure, cross-sector coordination, and the broader social and ethical context in which care occurs.

The use of the SWEET Institute's Four Layers of Transformation, conscious, pre-conscious, unconscious, and existential, offers a particularly valuable contribution. It acknowledges that systems are not merely mechanical constructs, but human ones: shaped by habits, beliefs, identities, and meaning. In this way, the book moves beyond traditional program manuals.

It becomes a guide to systemic and cultural transformation.

Much of contemporary mental health and social service delivery is characterized by fragmentation. There are multiple providers, multiple agencies, multiple documentation systems, and multiple and often conflicting priorities. For patients, this fragmentation can be bewildering. For clinicians, it can be exhausting; and for systems, it can be costly and ineffective. This book proposes an alternative: coherence through intentional design.

It offers tools to reduce duplication, align services, clarify roles, improve communication, and create pathways that are navigable for both providers and those they serve. These are not merely operational improvements. They are ethical imperatives.

In the emergency room, we often see the consequences of poorly designed systems in their most acute form. Patients who return repeatedly because continuity never existed. Individuals whose needs span housing, medical care, and mental health services, yet whose care remains siloed. Clinicians forced to make high-stakes decisions without access to integrated information or coordinated support. These are not isolated incidents. They are predictable outcomes of systems that lack integration; and what this book suggests, convincingly, is that these outcomes can be redesigned.

This book is not only for administrators or policymakers. It is for clinicians who want their work to extend beyond individual encounters, for supervisors seeking to support their teams more effectively, and for leaders responsible for building and sustaining programs. It is also for educators training the next generation of professionals, and anyone committed to aligning care with both evidence and ethics. It invites readers to expand their role from provider to designer, from participant to architect, and from responder to builder. At its core, it advances a simple but profound idea: Design is not neutral. The way we structure programs, allocate resources, define access, and coordinate care, shape who receives help, how they receive it, and whether it is effective. As such, to design a system is to make ethical decisions at scale, and this book equips readers to make those decisions more thoughtfully, more deliberately, and more effectively.

In conclusion, in emergency psychiatry, we often speak of stabilization, of helping individuals move from crisis to safety. However, stabilization is only the beginning. What follows depends on the systems into which individuals are discharged, referred, and supported. If those systems are fragmented, outcomes will be limited. If those systems are coherent, integrated, and human-centered, the possibilities expand.

Designing Care That Works is, ultimately, a book about expanding those possibilities. It challenges us to rethink not only how we deliver care, but how we construct the environments in which care becomes possible. In doing so, it offers something both practical and aspirational: a path toward systems that are not only more effective, but more just.

Jacob M. Appel, MD, JD, MPH, MPhil
Professor of Psychiatry and Medical Education
Icahn School of Medicine at Mount Sinai
Director of Ethics Education in Psychiatry
Assistant Director, Academy for Medicine & the Humanities
Emergency Room Psychiatrist, Mount Sinai Health System

Why This Book

There is a quiet truth in our field that rarely gets spoken out loud: Most clinicians, leaders, supervisors, and program directors were never taught how to design a program that actually works. As already stated, we teach diagnoses, treatment, documentation, ethics, and crisis response. We teach supervision, leadership, and organizational skills. However, the skill that determines whether any of that becomes meaningful in the real world is program design, and it is often left to guesswork, instinct, or trial by fire. The consequences are real. Programs collapse under their own complexity. Clinicians burn out, leaders become overwhelmed, and residents and clients fall through the cracks. Communities lose trust. Funders lose patience; and systems fail the exact people they were built to serve.

This book exists because that failure is preventable; because caring is not enough; and because design is what makes care possible. We wrote this book because clinicians deserve more than hope and hard work. They deserve clarity, structure, and a blueprint. We wrote it because leaders in social services and mental health are asked to solve problems that no one person, or even one discipline, can solve alone; and they deserve tools that match the complexity of the challenges they face. Lastly, we wrote it because program design is not to be reserved for administrators, consultants, or policymakers far from the front lines. It belongs to everyone in the system of care for the people we serve deserve systems that honor their humanity.

This book is for the clinician who wants their work to matter beyond the session. It is for the program director trying to build something that lasts; and it is for the leader who knows something in the system is broken, and wants to fix it. It is also for the social worker or nurse who sees gaps no one else sees. It is for the psychiatrist who knows medication alone will never be enough; and for the peer specialist whose insight could change everything if systems would listen. Lastly, it is for the administrator who wants to be bold, instead of bureaucratic; and for the funder who wants results rooted in dignity, equity, and truth.

Above all, this book is for the individuals, families, and communities who deserve better for our systems need transformation, not tweaks. As such, we stand on the shoulders of decades of community psychiatry, social work innovation, harm reduction, recovery movements, and trauma-informed care. The science is clear; the lived expertise is undeniable; and what we lack isn't passion; it's implementation. What we lack isn't compassion; it's structure; and what we lack isn't knowledge; it's integration.

This book bridges the gap between knowing, doing, sustaining, and transforming. It uses fiction, conversations, tools, scientific citations, reflections, and the SWEET 4-Layer Model to guide transformation at every level.

We wrote it because transformation ought to be systemic, human-centered, and intentional; and because the world is changing, and our systems need to evolve with it. We wrote it because the populations we serve aren't becoming simpler. They are becoming more layered, more interconnected, and more affected by systems we cannot control but need to respond to. Someone had to write this book, and we chose to.

In this vein, we wrote it for the field, for the workforce, and for the systems ready for a new path. We wrote it for the people who depend on these systems, and for the next generation of clinicians and leaders. Lastly, we wrote it because change is possible, when it is designed.

As such, this is more than a book. It is a beginning.

What This Book Is About

This book is about making care work, beyond theory, beyond papers, and beyond aspirational mission statements. It is about making care work in the messy, beautiful, and complex reality of everyday practice. It is about giving clinicians, supervisors, managers, directors, and leaders a step-by-step framework for designing programs that actually help people: programs that reduce suffering, restore dignity, close gaps rather than create new ones; and programs that last.

At its core, this book is a guide for turning good intentions into effective systems; and doing it in a way that is human, sustainable, and grounded in evidence.

This book is also about clarity, and about breaking program design down into simple, actionable steps using the Program Design Ladder, from Level 1 (micro-programs) to Level 5 (system transformation).

It is about tools, real tools you will use; real frameworks that simplify your thinking; real scripts that improve your interactions; and real dashboards that fit on one page.

Inside, you will find: logic models that make sense; implementation maps that guide your next step; and validation micro-scripts that transform engagement. You will also find data systems that don't overwhelm your staff; and evaluation tools that work even when capacity is limited. It is about people, instead of paperwork, for programs succeed or fail based on the relationships that hold them. Therefore, it teaches how to design programs that honor people experiencing homelessness; adolescents navigating trauma and identity; and older adults facing isolation and physical health complexity. It also teaches how to design programs that honor individuals living with SMI, SUD, or co-occurring disorders; Black, Latinx, LGBTQ+, and justice-involved communities; as well as families, caregivers, and front-line staff.

This is, then, neither a clinical book, nor a policy book, nor a leadership book. It is a people book, written for those who serve people. It is about systems, and how to change them. From small pilots to multi-site initiatives to system-wide transformation, you will learn how to start, how to build, how to scale, how to measure, how to sustain, how to replicate, and how to evolve. You will learn how to design systems that support clinicians rather than exhaust them; and systems that bring coherence, alignment, and purpose.

It is a book about transformation, and it uses the SWEET Institute's Four Layers of Transformation:

1. Conscious Layer – tools, behaviors, scripts, actions
2. Pre-Conscious Layer – patterns, habits, identity of teams
3. Unconscious Layer – beliefs, fears, emotional barriers
4. Existential Layer – meaning, purpose, culture, alignment

It shows how programs evolve when people evolve, and vice versa. In this spirit, it is about the possibility that: clinicians can become leaders of systems; supervisors can become designers of programs; a team can become a learning organization; a program can become a model; and a model can become a national movement. It is also about the possibility that our systems, which are currently, fractured, under-resourced, inequitable, and overwhelmed, can be redesigned with intention and humanity.

This book is about you, your voice, your leadership, your power to shape systems, and your ability to design care that works. It does not present itself as the final answer, but as the beginning of a new way of building programs across mental health, social services, supportive housing, community care, and every setting where people are trying to help other people.

If you work with humans, for humans, or on behalf of humans, this book is about you.

Part I — The Foundation: From Idea to Impact (Step-by-Step Basics)

Chapter 1: Why Programs Fail (and How Yours Won't): The Five Gaps

It was a Tuesday afternoon when Jay, a newly promoted program coordinator, realized the pilot project he had been so excited about was quietly falling apart. Clients were missing appointments, staff were unclear about priorities, and the dashboard meant to track progress hadn't been updated in weeks. In the corner of the room, Luis, the peer specialist, whispered to Amira, the program manager, 'I think we lost them before we even started.'

Conversation

Karen: *'This leads us to delve into the first sign a program is in trouble.'*

Mardoche: *'Yes. And it is when the people you serve feel like they're part of an experiment they didn't agree to.'*

Amira: *'And when the staff are working hard but rowing in different directions.'*

Luis: *'We all wanted it to work, but I guess wanting isn't a strategy.'*

Science Break

Research consistently shows that program failure in mental health and social services often stems from a small set of recurring issues, which we call the Five Gaps:

1. Clarity Gap – unclear goals, roles, and outcomes.
2. Fidelity Gap – inconsistent delivery of the model or intervention.
3. Equity Gap – neglecting cultural, linguistic, or accessibility needs.
4. Data Gap – absence of timely, relevant information to guide action.
5. Consistency Gap – unsustainable practices and staff turnover.

For example, the implementation science literature highlights that fidelity to evidence-based practices significantly predicts client outcomes (Aarons et al., 2011; Fixsen et al., 2005). Without fidelity monitoring, even well-designed programs lose impact.

Build It: Step-by-Step

Step 1: Define one measurable goal everyone can recite.
Step 2: Map the workflow and assign ownership for each step.
Step 3: Integrate equity considerations into every policy and form.
Step 4: Set up a simple, visible dashboard to track 3–5 key metrics.
Step 5: Establish weekly or biweekly team huddles to review progress.

Practice Lab

- **Reflection**: Which of the Five Gaps have you encountered in your own work?
- **Prompt**: Choose one gap and write down three concrete actions to close it in the next month.
- **Exercise**: Draft a one-page 'program clarity sheet' that lists your program's goal, target population, services, and success indicators.
- **Application**: Share your clarity sheet with your team and ask for feedback.

4-Layer Integration

1. **Conscious**: Clear Standard Operating Procedure (SOP), and visible metrics.
2. **Pre-conscious**: Regular reminders, defaults toward best practice.
3. **Unconscious**: Address staff narratives about 'why programs fail.'
4. **Existential**: Reconnect the team to the purpose behind the program.

References

- Aarons, G. A., Hurlburt, M., & Horwitz, S. M. (2011). Implementation science and child welfare: Bridging the gap between research and practice. *Child Welfare, 90*(2), 11–17.
- Fixsen, D. L., Naoom, S. F., Blase, K. A., Friedman, R. M., & Wallace, F. (2005). *Implementation research: A synthesis of the literature*. University of South Florida, Louis de la Parte Florida Mental Health Institute.

Chapter 2: The SWEET 4-Layer Transformation for Implementation

When Amira first heard about the SWEET 4-Layer Transformation, she imagined it was just another training buzzword. During a chaotic week, with two crises, a staff resignation, and a stakeholder call gone sideways, she found herself relying on it like a compass. She found it wasn't theory anymore; it was how she got through the week without losing the thread of the work.

SWEET 4-Layer Model

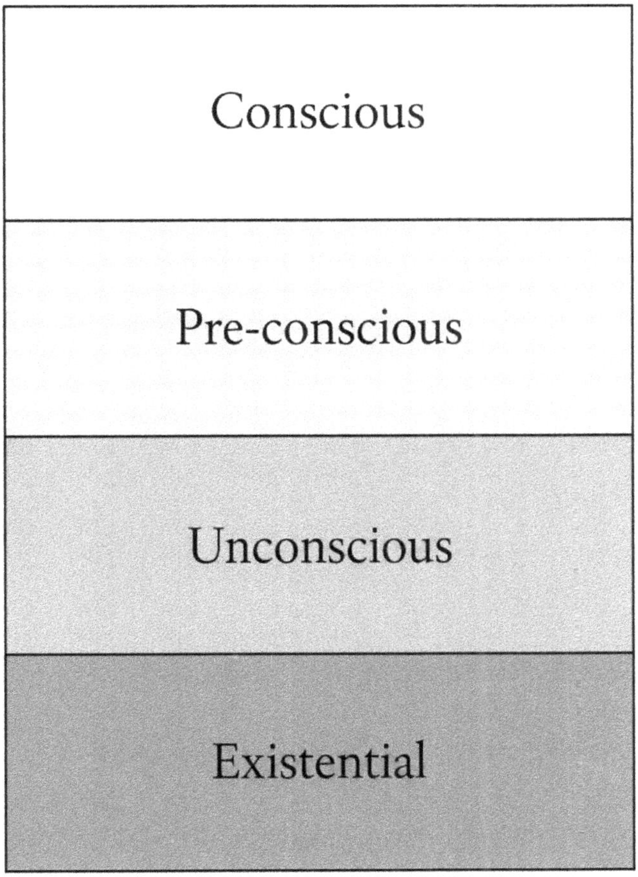

Conversation

Karen: *'The 4 layers aren't just for therapy or coaching. They're for program design, implementation, and leadership.'*

Mardoche: *'Right. Most programs operate at the conscious layer only. They focus on checklists, forms, SOPs. But without the other three layers, you're only treating the surface.'*

Luis: *'So the 4 layers are like working on the whole iceberg, not just the tip?'*

Karen: *'Exactly. Conscious, pre-conscious, unconscious, and existential: each one has its own set of tools, and together they change the whole system.'*

Science Break

The SWEET 4-Layer Transformation model is grounded in cognitive, behavioral, and psychoanalytic theories, as well as implementation science. The layers are:

1. **Conscious Layer** – Explicit actions, visible processes, and stated goals. Supported by behavioral activation research and procedural clarity.
2. **Pre-conscious Layer** – Cues, reminders, and subtle defaults that influence behavior without full awareness. Linked to habit formation and nudge theory (Thaler & Sunstein, 2008).
3. **Unconscious Layer** – Deep-seated beliefs, narratives, and transferences that drive engagement or resistance. Informed by psychoanalytic theory and schema therapy.
4. **Existential Layer** – Meaning, purpose, identity, and belonging. Supported by existential psychology and self-determination theory.

Addressing all four layers ensures that program design is not only effective but sustainable.

Build It: Step-by-Step

1. Map your program interventions across the four layers.
2. Identify at least one concrete tool or practice for each layer.
3. Train staff on how each layer shows up in daily work.
4. Integrate layer-based reflection into supervision and continuous Quality Improvement (CQI).
5. Measure both surface-level outcomes (conscious) and deeper changes (existential).

Practice Lab

- **Reflection**: Which layer do you naturally focus on in your current role?
- **Prompt**: Think of a time your team hit a barrier. Was it a conscious, pre-conscious, unconscious, or existential issue?
- **Exercise**: Take one existing workflow and add at least one intervention for each layer.
- **Application**: Use a 4-Layer Program Map template to review a program with your team.

4-Layer Integration

1. **Conscious**: Standard operating procedures, visible metrics, action plans.
2. **Pre-conscious**: Default scheduling, auto-reminders, workspace design.
3. **Unconscious**: Reflective supervision, addressing bias, transference, and countertransference.
4. **Existential**: Purpose statements, shared values, and belonging rituals.

References

- Deci, E. L., & Ryan, R. M. (2000). Self-determination theory and the facilitation of intrinsic motivation, social development, and well-being. *American Psychologist, 55*(1), 68–78.
- Thaler, R. H., & Sunstein, C. R. (2008). *Nudge: Improving decisions about health, wealth, and happiness*. Yale University Press.
- Young, J. E., Klosko, J. S., & Weishaar, M. E. (2003). *Schema therapy: A practitioner's guide*. Guilford Press.

Chapter 3: The Program Design Ladder (Level 1 → Level 5)

Jay stood in front of the whiteboard, staring at five uneven columns he had just drawn. He had been tasked with expanding a small pilot into a multi-site program, but the gap between where they were and where they needed to be felt like an ocean. Karen walked into the room and smiled: 'You're missing the ladder,' she said. 'Without the steps, you'll either leap and fall or stay stuck where you are.'

Conversation

Mardoche: *'The Program Design Ladder gives you a way to scale without breaking the program.'*

Karen: *'Each level is complete in itself. You can stop there or move up when you're ready.'*

Amira: *'So it's not about rushing to Level 5. It's about getting Level 1 right first.'*

Luis: *'And making sure each rung can actually hold the weight of the next.'*

Science Break

Scaling programs without a staged approach is one of the leading causes of failure in health and social services (Milat et al., 2016). The Program Design Ladder, adapted from implementation science frameworks, breaks growth into five levels:

1. **Level 1: Micro-Program** – A single intervention for a defined population, often a one-page design.
2. **Level 2: Pilot Program** – Small-scale, time-limited, with early fidelity and outcome checks.
3. **Level 3: Full Program** – SOPs, team roles, formal training, routine data collection.
4. **Level 4: Multi-Site Model** – Replication with fidelity tools, shared dashboards, and cross-site learning.
5. **Level 5: System Transformation** – Integrated policy, funding streams, and culture change across systems.

Program Design Ladder

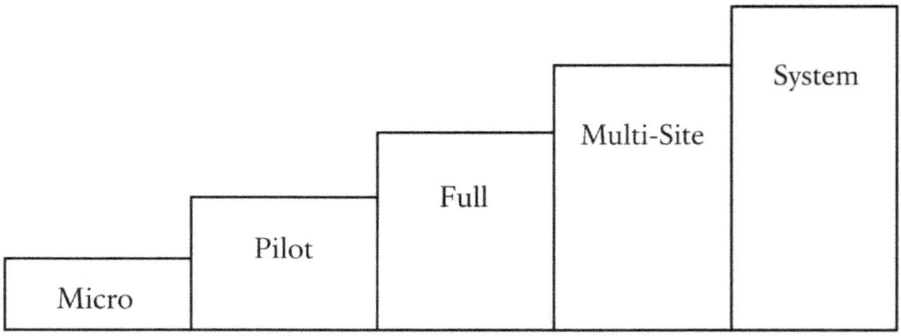

Research supports staged implementation for increasing fidelity, scalability, and sustainability (Fixsen et al., 2005; Moore et al., 2019).

Build It: Step-by-Step

1. Identify your current level honestly. Don't skip rungs.
2. Document what's needed to stabilize at your current level (fidelity, staff capacity, data).
3. Define the preparedness criteria for moving to the next level.
4. Build the next level using lessons and data from the current one.
5. Reassess after each transition. Growth isn't always linear.

Practice Lab

- **Reflection**: Which level best describes your current program?
- **Prompt**: What would it take to reach the next level in the next 6–12 months?
- **Exercise**: Map your program using the five-level ladder.

- **Application**: Identify three preparedness indicators for your next step.

4-Layer Integration

1. **Conscious**: Clear criteria for each level, visual ladder posted in workspaces.
2. **Pre-conscious**: Celebrate small wins at each rung to encourage momentum.
3. **Unconscious**: Address fears of scaling (loss of intimacy, role confusion).
4. **Existential**: Keep the purpose front-and-center to avoid mission drift.

References

- Fixsen, D. L., Naoom, S. F., Blase, K. A., Friedman, R. M., & Wallace, F. (2005). *Implementation research: A synthesis of the literature*. University of South Florida, Louis de la Parte Florida Mental Health Institute.
- Milat, A. J., King, L., Bauman, A. E., & Redman, S. (2013). The concept of scalability: Increasing the scale and potential impact of health promotion interventions. *Health Promotion International, 28*(3), 285–298.
- Moore, G. F., Evans, R. E., Hawkins, J., Littlecott, H. J., Melendez-Torres, G. J., Bonell, C., Murphy, S., & From complex interventions to complex systems: Sustainability and scale-up. (2019). *BMJ, 366*, l4893.

Chapter 4: Core Tools: Logic Model, Program Design Canvas, Engage360, Validation Micro-Scripts

Amira sat at her desk surrounded by a pile of half-finished program plans. Each one looked different, and none seemed to connect the dots from the problem they were trying to solve to the actual changes they hoped to see. Karen walked in holding a single sheet of paper: a logic model, and set it down. 'This,' she said, 'is how we keep the story straight from start to finish.'

Conversation

Karen: *'We have four tools that make any program design stronger: the Logic Model, the Program Design Canvas, the Engage360 Pathway, and Validation-First Micro-Scripts.'*

Mardoche: *'Think of them as your toolkit. Use them together and you'll see how the pieces fit.'*

Luis: *'I know about logic models, but what's the difference with the canvas?'*

Karen: *'The canvas is your quick visual. It's for clarity in the room. The logic model is for precision and funders. Engage360 gives you the engagement pathway, and validation-first micro-scripts shape the tone of every interaction.'*

Science Break

Evidence from implementation science shows that structured planning tools increase fidelity, alignment, and program impact (W. K. Kellogg Foundation, 2004; Milstein & Wetterhall, 1999).

The tools in this chapter support different stages of design and delivery:

1. **Logic Model**: links inputs, activities, outputs, and outcomes; provides a clear chain of reasoning.
2. **Program Design Canvas**: a one-page visual summarizing program goals, target population, services, measures, and equity considerations.

3. **Engage360 Pathway**: a sustainable change framework: Outreach & Trust, Safety & Stabilization, Activation & Skills, Integration & Independence.
4. **Validation-First Micro-Scripts**: short, scripted statements that communicate respect, empathy, and collaboration before moving into problem-solving.

These tools work best when used iteratively and integrated into staff workflows.

Build It: Step-by-Step

1. Draft a basic logic model for your program idea.
2. Translate it into a Program Design Canvas for quick reference.
3. Map services and workflows to the Engage360 Pathway.
4. Create 3–5 validation-first micro-scripts tailored to your population.
5. Review all four tools with your team and adjust for clarity and equity.

Practice Lab

- **Reflection**: Which of the four tools do you already use, and which are new to you?
- **Prompt**: How would your current program change if you consistently used all four tools?
- **Exercise**: Create a one-page Program Design Canvas for an existing or new program.
- **Application**: Role-play an intake interaction using a validation-first micro-script.

4-Layer Integration

1. **Conscious**: Completed tools embedded in workflows.
2. **Pre-conscious**: Visual reminders of the Engage360 stages posted in shared spaces.
3. **Unconscious**: Micro-scripts designed to counteract negative narratives.
4. **Existential**: Using validation to reinforce dignity, belonging, and purpose.

References

- Milstein, B., & Wetterhall, S. F. (1999). *A framework for program evaluation: A gateway to tools*. Centers for Disease Control and Prevention.
- W. K. Kellogg Foundation. (2004). *Logic model development guide*. W. K. Kellogg Foundation.

Chapter 5: Data-Lite, Impact-Strong: Outcomes, Proxies, and Simple Dashboards

Luis was never a 'data person.' He'd always seen dashboards as something for administrators and funders, not for frontline staff. One afternoon, after pulling up a simple color-coded spreadsheet showing which clients had not had a PCP visit in six months, he realized how quickly it could change his priorities, and theirs. By the end of the week, four clients had new appointments scheduled, and two had already gone.

Conversation

Karen: *'Data doesn't have to be heavy to be powerful.'*

Mardoche: *'The secret is knowing which outcomes matter and which proxies you can track easily.'*

Luis: *'So a proxy is like a stand-in for a bigger change?'*

Karen: *'Exactly. You might not be able to measure quality of life every week, but you can measure attendance at social activities, which is often a good proxy.'*

Science Break

Data systems in mental health and social services often fail because they're too complex for day-to-day use. Research supports the use of minimal viable dashboards, such as small sets of meaningful indicators that guide action without overwhelming staff (Bamberger et al., 2016).

Key definitions:

- **Outcome** – The actual change you want to see (e.g., reduced ER visits).
- **Proxy** – A simpler, more frequently measured indicator that predicts the outcome (e.g., kept medical appointments).
- **Dashboard** – A visual display of selected metrics that's easy to interpret and update.

Studies show that using visual dashboards increases adherence to evidence-based practices and improves outcomes when linked to team decision-making (Ivers et al., 2012).

Build It: Step-by-Step

1. Define 2–3 key outcomes for your program.
2. Identify at least one reliable proxy for each outcome.
3. Choose a simple format (spreadsheet, whiteboard, or app) for your dashboard.
4. Assign responsibility for updating it regularly.
5. Use the dashboard in team huddles to guide immediate action.

Practice Lab

- **Reflection**: What's one outcome in your program that feels hard to measure?
- **Prompt**: Identify a proxy you could track weekly that might predict that outcome.
- **Exercise**: Build a one-page dashboard for your team.
- **Application**: Use the dashboard in your next huddle and document any changes in decision-making.

4-Layer Integration

1. **Conscious**: A visible, up-to-date dashboard.
2. **Pre-conscious**: Automatic reminders to update metrics.
3. **Unconscious**: Reducing anxiety about 'data' by making it part of the routine.
4. **Existential**: Using data to reinforce purpose and shared wins.

References

- Bamberger, M., Vaessen, J., & Raimondo, E. (2016). *RealWorld evaluation: Working under budget, time, data, and political constraints* (2nd ed.). SAGE Publications.
- Ivers, N., Jamtvedt, G., Flottorp, S., Young, J. M., Odgaard-Jensen, J., French, S. D., O'Brien, M. A., Johansen, M., Grimshaw, J., & Oxman, A. D. (2012). Audit and feedback: Effects on professional practice and healthcare outcomes. *Cochrane Database of Systematic Reviews, 2012*(6), CD000259.

Chapter 6: The First 90 Days — From Idea to Operational Program

When Amira launched a new engagement program, the idea was simple, though implementation was not. Confusion, inconsistency, and resistance emerged quickly. By narrowing the scope, clarifying roles, and standardizing workflow, the program became operational by Day 90. It was not perfect, but it became real.

Conversation

Karen: *"Good ideas don't become good programs automatically."*

Mardoche: *"Programs become real through structure and repetition."*

Luis: *"The first 90 days determine survival."*

Science Break

Implementation science shows early success depends on feasibility, adoption, fidelity, and acceptability. Programs fail not from weak ideas, but from poor early structure.

Build It: Step-by-Step

1. Define the program in one page
2. Start small
3. Assign one owner
4. Standardize workflow
5. Use shared language
6. Create weekly rhythm
7. Track early indicators
8. Refine after use

Implementation Loop

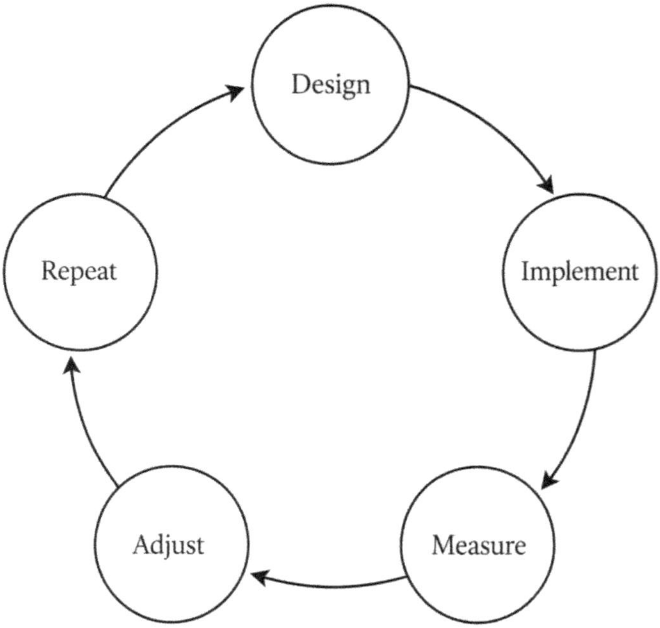

Practice Lab

- **Reflection**: What is unclear?
- **Prompt**: Can a new staff run this?
- **Exercise**: Build a 1-page plan.
- **Application**: Run once this week.

4-Layer Integration

1. **Conscious**: Structure
2. **Pre-conscious**: Habits
3. **Unconscious**: Resistance
4. **Existential**: Meaning

References

- Damschroder, L. J., Aron, D. C., Keith, R. E., Kirsh, S. R., Alexander, J. A., & Lowery, J. C. (2009). Fostering implementation of health services research findings into practice: A consolidated framework for advancing implementation science. Implementation Science, 4(1), 50.
- Fixsen, D. L., Naoom, S. F., Blase, K. A., Friedman, R. M., & Wallace, F. (2005). Implementation research: A synthesis of the literature. University of South Florida, Louis de la Parte Florida Mental Health Institute.
- Proctor, E., Silmere, H., Raghavan, R., Hovmand, P., Aarons, G., Bunger, A., Griffey, R., & Hensley, M. (2011). Outcomes for implementation research: Conceptual distinctions, measurement challenges, and research agenda. Administration and Policy in Mental Health and Mental Health Services Research, 38(2), 65–76.

Part II — The Program Design Ladder (from Basic to Complex)

Chapter 7: Level 1: Single-Page Micro-Program

When Dev, a high school social worker, was told to design an after-school stress management program, he imagined weeks of planning, grant proposals, and meetings. But his mentor, Amira, surprised him. 'We're starting with a single page,' she said. 'If you can't explain the program in one page, you don't yet know what it is.' Within two hours, Dev had a working plan, and by the next week, he had students attending, and enjoying the sessions.

Conversation

Karen: *'Level 1 is about clarity, speed, and testing your core idea.'*

Mardoche: *'A single-page micro-program can be implemented immediately while you refine the details.'*

Luis: *'It's also less intimidating. Staff feel like they can try it without a huge commitment.'*

Amira: *'And you learn faster because you're not bogged down in paperwork.'*

Science Break

Micro-programs, also known as 'minimum viable interventions,' are supported by rapid-cycle quality improvement research, which shows that small-scale, quickly implemented initiatives can yield significant insights and early wins (Langley et al., 2009). The benefits include:

- Low cost and minimal resources.
- Fast feedback from participants.
- Easier adaptation to different settings.
- Builds staff confidence and buy-in before larger rollouts.

Evidence suggests that testing small changes before scaling increases the success rate of complex program implementations.

Build It: Step-by-Step

1. Define the problem in one sentence.
2. Identify your target population.
3. Write down the single most important change you want to see.
4. List 3–5 core activities to achieve that change.
5. Choose 1–2 quick, easy-to-measure indicators of progress.
6. Pilot for 2–4 weeks and review feedback.

Practice Lab

- **Reflection**: What's one service idea you've been delaying because it feels too big?
- **Prompt**: How could you turn it into a one-page micro-program?
- **Exercise**: Use the Program Design Canvas to outline a micro-program.
- **Application**: Launch the program with a small group and gather feedback in real-time.

4-Layer Integration

1. **Conscious**: One-page plan visible to all team members.
2. **Pre-conscious**: Default to short, clear workflows.
3. **Unconscious**: Overcoming the belief that only 'big programs' have value.
4. **Existential**: Focusing on immediate, meaningful impact for participants.

References

Langley, G. J., Moen, R. D., Nolan, K. M., Nolan, T. W., Norman, C. L., & Provost, L. P. (2009). *The improvement guide: A practical approach to enhancing organizational performance* (2nd ed.). Jossey-Bass.

Chapter 8: Level 2: Designing and Running a Pilot Program

Tasha, a college mental health counselor, had an idea for a peer-led anxiety support group. Instead of launching it campus-wide, she decided to test it with a small group of students over six weeks. By the end of the pilot, attendance had grown, word of mouth was strong, and she had clear data on what was working, and what needed to change before expanding.

Conversation

Karen: *'Pilots are like rehearsals. They let you work out the kinks before the big performance.'*

Mardoche: *'And they help you secure buy-in from both staff and funders by showing early results.'*

Luis: *'Plus, you can fail safely. If something doesn't work, it's easier to pivot in a pilot than in a full rollout.'*

Amira: *'Pilots teach you things you'd never learn in planning meetings.'*

Science Break

Pilot programs are a core strategy in implementation science, serving as a bridge between concept and full-scale deployment (Craig et al., 2008). Benefits include:

- Testing feasibility and acceptability.
- Identifying implementation barriers.
- Refining workflows and materials.
- Generating preliminary outcome data.

Build It: Step-by-Step

1. Define the scope and duration (e.g., 90 days, one site, small cohort).
2. Set clear, measurable goals.

3. Identify your evaluation methods (outcomes and process measures).
4. Train staff or facilitators.
5. Launch with a limited group and gather both quantitative and qualitative feedback.
6. Analyze results and decide on next steps: refine, expand, or discontinue.

Practice Lab

- **Reflection**: What's one idea you could test as a pilot before committing to a full rollout?
- **Prompt**: How small could you make the pilot while still getting useful data?
- **Exercise**: Draft a 90-day pilot plan using the Program Design Canvas.
- **Application**: Identify at least three indicators you will track during the pilot.

4-Layer Integration

1. **Conscious**: Clear pilot plan and evaluation metrics.
2. **Pre-conscious**: Regular pilot review meetings to adjust quickly.
3. **Unconscious**: Reducing fear of failure by framing it as learning.
4. **Existential**: Using the pilot as a chance to deepen trust with participants.

References

- Craig, P., Dieppe, P., Macintyre, S., Michie, S., Nazareth, I., & Petticrew, M. (2008). Developing and evaluating complex interventions: The new Medical Research Council guidance. *BMJ, 337*, a1655.
- Eldridge, S. M., Lancaster, G. A., Campbell, M. J., Thabane, L., Hopewell, S., Coleman, C. L., & Bond, C. M. (2016). Defining feasibility and pilot studies in preparation for randomised controlled trials: Development of a conceptual framework. *Pilot and Feasibility Studies, 2*(1), 1–12.

Chapter 9: Level 3: Building a Full Program

After a successful 90-day pilot, Amira's reentry program for justice-involved individuals was ready to expand. She now needed dedicated staff, standard operating procedures, a consistent referral pathway, and a formal training plan. The program was moving from an experiment to a fully integrated service, and the stakes and the impact were higher than ever.

Conversation

Karen: '*Level 3 is where your program becomes part of the organization's identity.*'

Mardoche: '*It also means it has to survive beyond the enthusiasm of the launch team.*'

Luis: '*That's where SOPs, training, and data systems come in so it's not just dependent on a few individuals.*'

Amira: '*And it's where you start tracking outcomes consistently for accountability and improvement.*'

Science Break

Full programs require a blend of operational stability and adaptive learning. Implementation science identifies key drivers for success at this stage: competency drivers (training, coaching, fidelity assessment), organization drivers (data systems, administrative support), and leadership drivers (technical and adaptive leadership) (Fixsen et al., 2005).

Level 3 also demands clear role definitions, reliable funding streams, and the integration of equity and cultural humility into all processes.

Build It: Step-by-Step

1. Finalize SOPs for all core workflows.
2. Establish a formal training and onboarding program for staff.

3. Set up routine data collection and reporting.
4. Secure a stable funding source.
5. Integrate the program into organizational policies and strategic plans.
6. Conduct quarterly CQI cycles.

Practice Lab

- **Reflection**: What's one area of your program that still depends too much on one person's knowledge?
- **Prompt**: How could you systematize that knowledge into SOPs or training?
- **Exercise**: Create or update your program's onboarding checklist.
- **Application**: Schedule your first quarterly CQI review.

4-Layer Integration

1. **Conscious**: SOPs, training manuals, and dashboards.
2. **Pre-conscious**: Default scheduling for onboarding and review.
3. **Unconscious**: Building a culture that supports the program's mission.
4. **Existential**: Aligning the program's work with the organization's core purpose.

References

Fixsen, D. L., Naoom, S. F., Blase, K. A., Friedman, R. M., & Wallace, F. (2005). *Implementation research: A synthesis of the literature*. University of South Florida, Louis de la Parte Florida Mental Health Institute.

Chapter 10: Level 4: Designing for Multi-Site Implementation

When the youth mental health program that started in one high school expanded to five campuses, Amira quickly learned that what worked in one site didn't automatically translate to another. Staff training had to be standardized, data needed to be comparable across locations, and the core model had to be preserved while allowing for local adaptation.

Conversation

Karen: *'Multi-site is where you prove your program can be both consistent and flexible.'*

Mardoche: *'You need strong fidelity tools, but also respect for each site's unique context.'*

Luis: *'It's like a recipe. You keep the core ingredients, but you can adjust the seasoning for local taste.'*

Amira: *'And communication between sites is just as important as communication within them.'*

Science Break

Multi-site implementation requires balancing fidelity and adaptation. Research shows that both are critical. Programs that adapt without losing their core components have higher effectiveness across diverse settings (Durlak & DuPre, 2008).

- A clearly defined core model.
- Standardized training and onboarding.
- Cross-site data systems.
- Regular learning collaboratives.
- Structured adaptation guidelines.

Build It: Step-by-Step

1. Define the non-negotiable elements of your model.
2. Develop standardized training and fidelity monitoring tools.

3. Create shared data definitions and a central dashboard.
4. Establish regular cross-site meetings or learning sessions.
5. Document approved adaptations and lessons learned.
6. Celebrate site-specific innovations that align with the core model.

Practice Lab

- **Reflection**: What are the core elements of your program that should never change?
- **Prompt**: Where could local adaptation improve outcomes without compromising fidelity?
- **Exercise**: Draft a 'fidelity and flexibility' checklist for your program.
- **Application**: Host your first cross-site learning collaborative.

4-Layer Integration

1. **Conscious**: Standardized training, core model documents, and dashboards.
2. **Pre-conscious**: Built-in rhythms for cross-site sharing.
3. **Unconscious**: Encouraging curiosity about other sites' successes.
4. **Existential**: Reinforcing the shared mission that unites all sites.

References

Durlak, J. A., & DuPre, E. P. (2008). Implementation matters: A review of research on the influence of implementation on program outcomes and the factors affecting implementation. *American Journal of Community Psychology, 41*(3–4), 327–350.

Chapter 11: Level 5: System Transformation & Ecosystem-Level Change

When Miguel's city launched a coordinated homelessness response integrating health, housing, and justice systems, he realized they weren't just running a program anymore. They were changing how the entire system operated. Multiple agencies shared data, policies were rewritten, and funding streams were aligned. It was no longer about one team's success. It was about building a new way of working for an entire community.

Conversation

Karen: *'System transformation means your work influences policy, funding, and culture.'*

Mardoche: *'It's where you address root causes, not just symptoms.'*

Luis: *'And where you need strong political will and long-term commitment.'*

Amira: *'This is where leadership becomes about alignment across entire sectors.'*

Science Break

System transformation occurs when interventions are embedded into the structures, policies, and culture of organizations and communities. Research on collective impact and systems change emphasizes five conditions: common agenda, shared measurement, mutually reinforcing activities, continuous communication, and backbone support (Kania & Kramer, 2011).

Transformations often involve:

- Policy change.
- Cross-sector funding alignment.
- Data-sharing agreements.
- Workforce development at scale.
- Community engagement and leadership from affected populations.

Build It: Step-by-Step

1. Establish a common vision and goals across sectors.
2. Create shared measurement systems.
3. Align funding streams to support integrated work.
4. Build a backbone organization or coordinating body.
5. Engage communities in leadership roles.
6. Institutionalize policies and practices so they survive leadership changes.

Practice Lab

- **Reflection**: Which systems do you need to influence for your work to have lasting impact?
- **Prompt**: What would policy alignment look like in your area of focus?
- **Exercise**: Map key stakeholders and their influence on system-level decisions.
- **Application**: Propose one cross-sector initiative that could address a root cause of your population's challenges.

4-Layer Integration

1. **Conscious**: Shared data dashboards, policy documents, formal agreements.
2. **Pre-conscious**: Regular interagency meetings and communication channels.
3. **Unconscious**: Building trust across sectors and reframing narratives about the problem.
4. **Existential**: Fostering a shared sense of responsibility and possibility for systemic change.

ences

J., & Kramer, M. (2011). Collective impact. *Stanford Social ion Review, 9*(1), 36–41.

Chapter 12: Engagement That Lasts — From First Contact to Long-Term Retention

James had been referred five times. Each time, he came for intake, and never returned.

He has been to different clinicians and different programs; yet the outcome has been the same.

"Non-compliant," someone wrote.

When Maria met him, she noticed something different. He wasn't resistant; rather, he was uncertain. So, she asked, *"Tell me what would make this worth your time."*

No one had asked him that before. He stayed longer. Then he came back. Then he engaged. Nothing about the program had changed; but the engagement had.

Conversation

Karen: *"Programs don't fail because they don't exist. They fail because people don't stay."*

Mardoche: *"Access is not engagement."*

Luis: *"And engagement is not retention."*

Amira: *"Engagement is a sequence, not a moment."*

Science Break

Engagement predicts outcomes across mental health and social services. Early sessions determine retention; and therapeutic alliance is one of the strongest predictors of outcomes.

- Is this safe?
- Is this useful?
- Is this worth my time?

If not, they disengage.

Build It: Step-by-Step

1. Design the first contact intentionally.
2. Make the program understandable.
3. Create early wins.
4. Standardize validation.
5. Build predictable structure.
6. Track engagement.
7. Address drop-off quickly.
8. Adapt without losing structure.

Practice Lab

- **Reflection**: Where do people drop off?
- **Prompt**: What do the first 5 minutes feel like?
- **Exercise**: Design a first contact script.
- **Application**: Track engagement this week.

4-Layer Integration

1. **Conscious**: Scripts, structure, workflow
2. **Pre-conscious**: Habits, consistency
3. **Unconscious**: Bias, fear, resistance
4. **Existential**: Meaning, dignity, purpose

References

- Deci, E. L., & Ryan, R. M. (2000). Self-determination theory and the facilitation of intrinsic motivation, social development, and well-being. *American Psychologist, 55*(1), 68–78.
- Horvath, A. O., & Symonds, B. D. (1991). Relation between working alliance and outcome in psychotherapy: A meta-analysis. *Journal of Counseling Psychology, 38*(2), 139–149.

- Norcross, J. C., & Wampold, B. E. (2011). Evidence-based therapy relationships: Research conclusions and clinical practices. *Psychotherapy, 48*(1), 98–102.
- Swift, J. K., & Greenberg, R. P. (2012). Premature discontinuation in adult psychotherapy: A meta-analysis. *Journal of Consulting and Clinical Psychology, 80*(4), 547–559.

Part III — Populations & Settings (Applied Scenarios)

Chapter 13: Older Adults & Geriatric Mental Health

Mr. Greene, an 82-year-old veteran, had been living alone since his wife passed away. His primary care visits were sporadic, and he had fallen twice in the last year. When the community health team visited, they discovered he hadn't been taking his medications regularly because the pill bottles were hard to open. A simple change, switching to blister packs, reduced his confusion and helped him stay on track.

Conversation

Karen: *'Older adults often face overlapping challenges: physical health, mental health, and social isolation.'*

Mardoche: *'And small, practical interventions can have an outsized impact.'*

Luis: *'Like changing packaging or connecting someone to a social group. It's not always about a new medication.'*

Amira: *'It's about designing programs that meet both medical and social needs.'*

Science Break

Older adults with mental health needs often experience higher rates of hospitalization and functional decline. Integrated care models that address physical, mental, and social determinants have been shown to improve outcomes and reduce costs (Counsell et al., 2007).

Common geriatric psychiatry program priorities include:

- Fall prevention.
- Medication reconciliation.
- Depression and cognitive screening.
- Caregiver support.
- Social engagement opportunities.

Build It: Step-by-Step

1. Screen for both mental and physical health needs.
2. Identify environmental risks (e.g., fall hazards).
3. Simplify medication management.
4. Connect to social and community resources.
5. Engage caregivers as partners in care.
6. Monitor and adjust interventions regularly.

Practice Lab

- **Reflection**: What barriers to care do older adults in your community face?
- **Prompt**: Which could be addressed with low-cost interventions?
- **Exercise**: Design a one-page program for fall prevention and social engagement.
- **Application**: Pilot the program with five older adults and track outcomes over three months.

4-Layer Integration

1. **Conscious**: Checklists for fall prevention and medication review.
2. **Pre-conscious**: Home visits that naturally incorporate safety scans.
3. **Unconscious**: Building trust with older adults who may fear losing independence.
4. **Existential**: Supporting dignity, purpose, and connection in later life.

References

Counsell, S. R., Callahan, C. M., Buttar, A. B., Clark, D. O., & Frank, K. I. (2007). Geriatric care management for low-income seniors: A randomized controlled trial. *JAMA, 298*(22), 2623–2633.

Chapter 14: Children & Families

Eight-year-old Mia had been having trouble at school: frequent absences, difficulty focusing, and sudden outbursts in class. When the school social worker visited her home, she discovered that Mia's family had been evicted twice in the past year and were living in a relative's basement. Stability at home, not just behavior plans at school, was the real key to supporting Mia's success.

Conversation

Karen: *'Programs for children have to include the family; otherwise, we're treating symptoms, not causes.'*

Mardoche: *'Exactly. And we have to look at housing, food security, and parental support alongside the child's needs.'*

Luis: *'It's a whole-ecosystem approach: school, home, community.'*

Amira: *'And it has to be flexible, because kids' needs change fast.'*

Science Break

Child and family mental health programs are most effective when they integrate school, home, and community resources. Research shows that multi-component interventions, such as combining academic support, behavioral interventions, and family engagement, lead to better outcomes than single-focus programs (Weare & Nind, 2011).

Key priorities include:

- Early identification and intervention.
- Family engagement and empowerment.
- Trauma-informed practices.
- Coordination between school, healthcare, and community agencies.
- Culturally responsive approaches.

Build It: Step-by-Step

1. Conduct a comprehensive assessment including family and environmental factors.
2. Develop an integrated plan linking school, home, and community supports.
3. Provide trauma-informed training for all staff.
4. Offer flexible service delivery (e.g., home visits, telehealth).
5. Review and adapt the plan regularly as needs change.

Practice Lab

- **Reflection**: How well do your current programs integrate family needs with child-focused services?
- **Prompt**: Which community partners could strengthen your program's impact?
- **Exercise**: Create a service map linking school, home, and community supports for one child.
- **Application**: Pilot a family engagement strategy and track changes in attendance and behavior.

4-Layer Integration

1. **Conscious**: Service coordination plans and communication logs.
2. **Pre-conscious**: Default to family-inclusive scheduling.
3. **Unconscious**: Addressing staff assumptions about family engagement.
4. **Existential**: Supporting a family's hope and vision for their child's future.

References

Weare, K., & Nind, M. (2011). Mental health promotion and problem prevention in schools: What does the evidence say? *Health Promotion International, 26*(Suppl. 1), i29–i69.

Chapter 15: Adolescents & School Mental Health

Dev, a 15-year-old high school student, had been skipping classes and getting into fights. When the school counselor finally met with him, she learned his family had been struggling financially, and Dev felt hopeless about his future. Instead of punitive measures, the school launched a tiered support program: peer mentoring, skills groups, and counseling, which led to improved attendance and a drop in disciplinary incidents.

Conversation

Karen: *'Adolescents need programs that recognize their developmental stage: identity, autonomy, and belonging.'*

Mardoche: *'And schools are a primary access point for mental health support at this age.'*

Luis: *'The challenge is balancing confidentiality with parental involvement.'*

Amira: *'And making sure interventions are culturally responsive and strengths-based.'*

Science Break

School-based mental health programs for adolescents can improve academic performance, reduce behavioral problems, and increase help-seeking behavior. Tiered systems of support, such as Multi-Tiered Systems of Support (MTSS) and Positive Behavioral Interventions and Supports (PBIS), are evidence-based frameworks for addressing a range of needs (Sugai & Horner, 2009).

Effective components include:

- Early identification and screening.
- Tiered interventions (universal, targeted, intensive).
- Social-emotional learning (SEL) programs.
- Peer support and mentoring.

- Collaboration between school staff, families, and community providers.

Build It: Step-by-Step

1. Implement universal screening for emotional and behavioral concerns.
2. Establish tiered support pathways.
3. Train school staff in trauma-informed and culturally responsive practices.
4. Incorporate peer-led initiatives.
5. Evaluate program outcomes in both academic and well-being domains.

System Integration Map

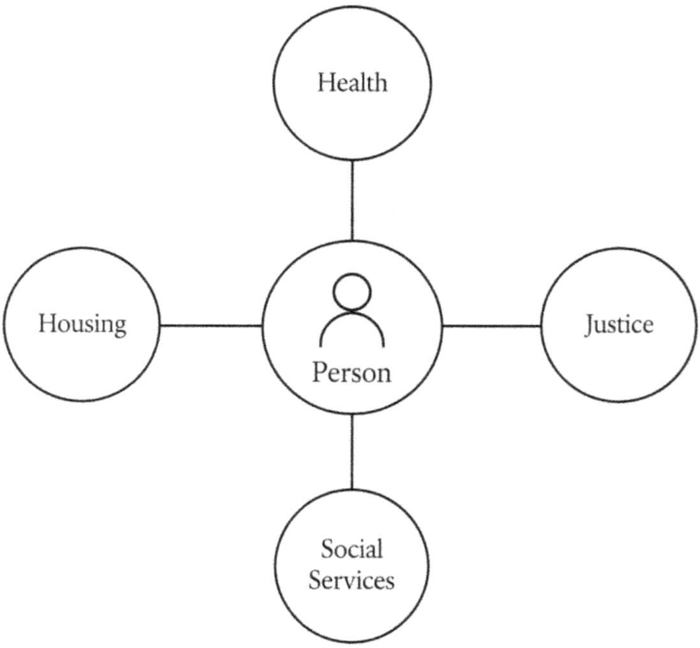

Practice Lab

- **Reflection**: What mental health needs are most common among adolescents in your setting?
- **Prompt**: Which supports could be integrated into the school day to increase accessibility?
- **Exercise**: Design a three-tier support framework for your school.
- **Application**: Pilot one targeted intervention and track its impact over a semester.

4-Layer Integration

1. **Conscious**: Tiered support plans and screening tools.
2. **Pre-conscious**: Visual reminders of coping skills throughout the school.
3. **Unconscious**: Building positive identity narratives for students.
4. **Existential**: Supporting a sense of purpose and belonging in the school community.

References

Sugai, G., & Horner, R. H. (2009). Responsiveness-to-intervention and school-wide positive behavior supports: Integration of multi-tiered system approaches. *Exceptionality, 17*(4), 223–237.

Chapter 16: College Mental Health & Campus Well-Being

Tasha, a junior in college, had been struggling with panic attacks before exams. She knew the counseling center existed but believed the waitlist was too long to bother trying. When her university implemented a stepped care model, she was able to get a same-week single-session appointment, followed by a brief skills group, and later, individual counseling. Her symptoms improved, and she felt supported without missing class.

Conversation

Karen: *'College students need accessible, flexible mental health options.'*

Mardoche: *'Stepped care models are perfect for this. They match intensity of care to the student's needs.'*

Luis: *'And they can help reduce wait times for higher-need students.'*

Amira: *'It's about balancing demand with capacity while maintaining quality.'*

Science Break

College mental health programs face rising demand, with anxiety and depression being the most common concerns (ACHA, 2022). Stepped care models, which provide a range of services from self-help to intensive therapy, can improve access and efficiency without sacrificing outcomes (Bower & Gilbody, 2005).

Key elements include:

- Initial triage and assessment.
- Multiple levels of intervention.
- Rapid access to low-intensity supports.
- Clear pathways to higher-intensity care.
- Integration with academic and campus life resources.

Build It: Step-by-Step

- Conduct a needs assessment of the student population.
- Design a stepped care framework tailored to available resources.
- Train staff in triage and brief interventions.
- Offer a range of modalities (in-person, online, group, peer-led).
- Track utilization and outcomes to adjust service levels.

Practice Lab

- **Reflection**: What are the main barriers to care for students on your campus?
- **Prompt**: Which lower-intensity supports could you implement quickly?
- **Exercise**: Map your current services to a stepped care model.
- **Application**: Pilot one new step in the model and collect feedback from students.

4-Layer Integration

- **Conscious**: Clear service maps and referral protocols.
- **Pre-conscious**: Prompts in student portals to encourage help-seeking.
- **Unconscious**: Addressing stigma about mental health in campus culture.
- **Existential**: Supporting students' sense of belonging and purpose in college life.

References

- American College Health Association. (2022). *National College Health Assessment*. American College Health Association.
- Bower, P., & Gilbody, S. (2005). Stepped care in psychological therapies: Access, effectiveness and efficiency. *British Journal of Psychiatry, 186*(1), 11–17.

Chapter 17: Homelessness & Serious Mental Illness

Ms. Ortiz had been living in a shelter for three years, cycling in and out of the emergency department. She had a diagnosis of schizophrenia and struggled to maintain consistent treatment due to lost medications and frequent moves. When the SWEET Team began visiting her weekly, they started with simple steps: replacing her lost ID, ensuring she had a phone, and validating her experiences. Over time, she began attending psychiatric appointments, taking her medication regularly, and engaging in social activities.

Conversation

Karen: *'For people experiencing homelessness with SMI, engagement has to come before anything else.'*

Mardoche: *'That's why the Engage360 pathway starts with Outreach & Trust: It's the foundation.'*

Luis: *'You can't jump to med adherence if someone doesn't even feel safe talking to you.'*

Amira: *'And safety isn't just about physical space. It's emotional safety too.'*

Science Break

People experiencing homelessness with serious mental illness have higher rates of hospitalization, incarceration, and mortality (Fazel et al., 2014). Evidence supports low-barrier, person-centered, and trauma-informed approaches that prioritize engagement and basic needs before clinical interventions (SAMHSA, 2014).

The Engage360 Pathway includes:

- **Stage 1: Outreach & Trust** – Validation-first scripts, immediate needs, quick wins.
- **Stage 2: Safety & Stabilization** – Safety planning, medical and psychiatric linkage.

- **Stage 3: Activation & Skills** – Medication adherence supports, behavioral activation.
- **Stage 4: Integration & Independence** – Peer-led groups, relapse prevention, alumni follow-up.

Build It: Step-by-Step

1. Identify target population using clear criteria.
2. Assign staff with training in MI, trauma-informed care, and harm reduction.
3. Implement Engage360 stages, tracking progress for each participant.
4. Use quick wins to build trust early.
5. Link to ongoing medical, psychiatric, and housing supports.
6. Monitor outcomes and adjust interventions.

Practice Lab

- **Reflection**: What barriers have you encountered in engaging people experiencing homelessness with SMI?
- **Prompt**: What quick wins could you offer within the first two weeks of contact?
- **Exercise**: Map a participant's journey through the Engage360 pathway.
- **Application**: Pilot the pathway with three individuals and review results after 90 days.

4-Layer Integration

1. **Conscious**: Stage-based engagement plans and progress notes.
2. **Pre-conscious**: Defaults to early trust-building actions.
3. **Unconscious**: Addressing staff assumptions about readiness.
4. **Existential**: Reinforcing dignity, belonging, and hope.

References

- Fazel, S., Geddes, J. R., & Kushel, M. (2014). The health of homeless people in high-income countries: Descriptive epidemiology, health consequences, and clinical and policy recommendations. *The Lancet, 384*(9953), 1529–1540.
- Substance Abuse and Mental Health Services Administration. (2014). *Trauma-informed care in behavioral health services*. U.S. Department of Health and Human Services.

Chapter 18: Justice-Involved Reentry & Community Reintegration

Miguel had just been released from jail after serving a six-month sentence for a probation violation. He had no ID, no housing, and no steady access to his prescribed medication for bipolar disorder. A reentry program met him at the gate, arranged a temporary housing placement, helped him apply for benefits, and connected him to a psychiatric provider within a week. By the end of his first month out, Miguel was attending peer support groups and had started a job readiness program.

Conversation

Karen: *'The first 30 days after release are critical for stability and preventing recidivism.'*

Mardoche: *'That's when engagement, connection to services, and medication continuity matter most.'*

Luis: *'A warm handoff at the gate changes the entire trajectory.'*

Amira: *'And coordination with probation or parole can reduce stress and confusion for the participant.'*

Science Break

Justice-involved individuals face high risks of relapse, homelessness, and re-incarceration during reentry. Research shows that integrated reentry programs, addressing housing, employment, health care, and behavioral health, reduce recidivism and improve health outcomes (Mallik-Kane & Visher, 2008).

Best practices include:

- Pre-release planning.
- Immediate post-release contact.
- Identification and benefits reinstatement.
- Rapid linkage to medical and mental health services.
- Peer mentorship from individuals with lived experience.

Build It: Step-by-Step

1. Begin engagement before release when possible.
2. Provide a warm handoff on the day of release.
3. Address identification, benefits, and housing immediately.
4. Link to health and mental health services within 7 days.
5. Offer peer and community support.
6. Track progress for at least 90 days.

Practice Lab

- **Reflection**: What partnerships are essential for a successful reentry program in your area?
- **Prompt**: Which services could you link participants to within the first week?
- **Exercise**: Map a 30-day reentry plan for a hypothetical participant.
- **Application**: Pilot the plan with one participant and track outcomes.

4-Layer Integration

1. **Conscious**: Written reentry plans and service checklists.
2. **Pre-conscious**: Defaults to early engagement and benefit reinstatement.
3. **Unconscious**: Building trust with participants who may be wary of systems.
4. **Existential**: Supporting a sense of possibility and self-determination.

References

Mallik-Kane, K., & Visher, C. A. (2008). *Health and prisoner reentry: How physical, mental, and substance abuse conditions shape the process of reintegration*. Urban Institute Justice Policy Center.

Chapter 19: LGBTQ+-Affirming Program Design

Rae, a 19-year-old transgender woman, had avoided health care for years due to previous experiences of discrimination. When she finally connected with an LGBTQ+-affirming program, she was greeted by staff trained in inclusive practices, saw her pronouns respected without question, and was connected to both gender-affirming care and mental health support. Within months, she reported reduced anxiety and a stronger sense of belonging.

Conversation

Karen: *'Affirmation isn't just about tolerance. It's about active inclusion.'*

Mardoche: *'That means policies, training, and environments that signal safety from the first contact.'*

Luis: *'Even small changes, like inclusive intake forms, can make a big difference.'*

Amira: *'And programs need to connect people to affirming health care providers and community resources.'*

Science Break

LGBTQ+ individuals face higher rates of mental health challenges, including depression, anxiety, and suicide risk, often due to minority stress and discrimination (Meyer, 2003). Affirming programs that integrate culturally competent care, community connection, and advocacy improve engagement and outcomes (Craig et al., 2015).

Key program components:

- Staff training in LGBTQ+ cultural competence.
- Inclusive policies and intake procedures.
- Safe, visible signs of affirmation in physical spaces.
- Connections to affirming medical and mental health providers.

- Peer support and community-building opportunities.

Build It: Step-by-Step

1. Review and revise policies for inclusivity.
2. Provide comprehensive LGBTQ+ cultural competence training.
3. Audit physical and virtual spaces for visible affirmation.
4. Develop a network of affirming service providers.
5. Facilitate peer-led support and social programs.

Practice Lab

- **Reflection**: How affirming are your current programs for LGBTQ+ individuals?
- **Prompt**: What immediate changes could signal greater safety and inclusion?
- **Exercise**: Conduct an inclusivity audit of your program.
- **Application**: Implement one new affirmation practice and gather participant feedback.

4-Layer Integration

1. **Conscious**: Inclusive forms, policies, and procedures.
2. **Pre-conscious**: Visual cues of safety and affirmation.
3. **Unconscious**: Addressing staff biases and assumptions.
4. **Existential**: Supporting identity, belonging, and self-worth.

References

- Craig, S. L., Austin, A., & Alessi, E. J. (2015). Affirmative cognitive-behavioral therapy with transgender youth: Integrating clinical expertise, client perspectives, and the best available research. *Professional Psychology: Research and Practice, 46*(1), 21–29.
- Meyer, I. H. (2003). Prejudice, social stress, and mental health in lesbian, gay, and bisexual populations: Conceptual issues and research evidence. *Psychological Bulletin, 129*(5), 674–697.

Chapter 20: Black Mental Health: Healing, Identity & Systems

Aaliyah, a 34-year-old Black mother of two, sought therapy after experiencing workplace discrimination and chronic anxiety. Her previous attempts at care had left her feeling unheard and misunderstood. When she joined a program specifically designed for Black mental health, she was paired with a culturally competent therapist, participated in group sessions centered on racial identity, and learned coping strategies rooted in both evidence-based practices and cultural strengths. Over time, she reported improved mental health and a renewed sense of empowerment.

Conversation

Karen: *'Addressing Black mental health means understanding historical and systemic factors.'*

Mardoche: *'Including racism, discrimination, and internalized oppression.'*

Luis: *'It also means recognizing resilience and cultural strengths.'*

Amira: *'And designing programs that affirm identity and provide safe spaces.'*

Science Break

Black Americans experience disparities in access to and quality of mental health care, influenced by systemic racism, economic inequities, and stigma (Hankerson et al., 2015). Programs that integrate culturally adapted interventions, address social determinants, and include community partnerships show improved engagement and outcomes.

Key program priorities:

- Cultural competence and humility training for staff.
- Inclusion of Black clinicians and peer providers.
- Addressing social determinants such as housing, employment, and justice involvement.

- Community-based outreach and engagement.
- Incorporating culturally relevant coping strategies and narratives.

Build It: Step-by-Step

1. Engage community stakeholders in program design.
2. Provide staff training on cultural humility and anti-racism.
3. Offer services in community-based settings.
4. Address systemic barriers through advocacy and partnerships.
5. Collect and analyze outcomes data stratified by race and ethnicity.

Practice Lab

- **Reflection**: How does your current program address systemic and cultural factors impacting Black mental health?
- **Prompt**: What community partnerships could strengthen your program?
- **Exercise**: Design a culturally adapted intervention for your setting.
- **Application**: Pilot the intervention and gather feedback from participants.

4-Layer Integration

1. **Conscious**: Culturally adapted program materials.
2. **Pre-conscious**: Representation in imagery and staffing.
3. **Unconscious**: Addressing internalized oppression and bias.
4. **Existential**: Affirming identity, resilience, and collective healing.

References

Hankerson, S. H., Suite, D., & Bailey, R. K. (2015). Treatment disparities among African American men with depression. *Journal of Health Care for the Poor and Underserved, 26*(1), 21–34.

Chapter 21: Latinx Mental Health & Cultural Strengths

Miguel, a 42-year-old construction worker, had been feeling depressed for months but avoided seeking help because he feared being judged and did not know of any Spanish-speaking providers. When a community health center launched a Latino-focused mental health program, Miguel was matched with a bilingual counselor, received culturally adapted therapy, and joined a support group where members shared similar life experiences. He began to feel less alone and more hopeful.

Conversation

Karen: *'Language access is the first barrier we have to address.'*

Mardoche: *'But cultural competence goes beyond language. It's about understanding values, traditions, and migration experiences.'*

Luis: *'And building trust through community partnerships and consistent presence.'*

Amira: *'It's also important to involve families whenever possible.'*

Science Break

Latino communities face disparities in mental health service use due to language barriers, stigma, immigration concerns, and lack of culturally competent care (Alegría et al., 2008). Programs that provide bilingual services, integrate family involvement, and partner with trusted community organizations have higher engagement and retention rates.

Key elements of effective programs:

- Bilingual and bicultural staff.
- Culturally adapted interventions.
- Family-inclusive approaches.
- Partnerships with faith-based and community organizations.
- Education to reduce stigma and increase awareness.

Build It: Step-by-Step

1. Hire and train bilingual/bicultural staff.
2. Adapt materials and interventions for cultural relevance.
3. Partner with trusted community organizations.
4. Incorporate family engagement strategies.
5. Monitor and evaluate outcomes with input from the community.

Practice Lab

- **Reflection**: How accessible are your current services to Latino communities?
- **Prompt**: Which community partnerships could improve trust and engagement?
- **Exercise**: Create a culturally adapted outreach plan.
- **Application**: Implement the plan and track engagement rates over three months.

4-Layer Integration

1. **Conscious**: Bilingual materials and service information.
2. **Pre-conscious**: Physical spaces reflecting Latino cultures.
3. **Unconscious**: Addressing staff biases and assumptions.
4. **Existential**: Affirming identity, family, and community belonging.

References

Alegría, M., Carson, N. J., Gonçalves, M., & Keefe, K. (2011). Disparities in treatment for substance use disorders and co-occurring disorders for ethnic/racial minority youth. *Journal of the American Academy of Child & Adolescent Psychiatry, 50*(1), 22–31.

Chapter 22: Substance Use, Addiction & Harm Reduction

John, a 28-year-old man experiencing homelessness, had been using opioids for over a decade. He had been through multiple detox programs but relapsed each time. When he connected with a harm reduction program, instead of being pressured to quit immediately, he was offered medication for opioid use disorder (MOUD), clean supplies, and a safe space to talk. Over time, John reduced his use, stabilized his housing, and began planning for long-term recovery.

Conversation

Karen: *'Harm reduction meets people where they are, without judgment.'*

Mardoche: *'And it increases the chances they'll engage in services over time.'*

Luis: *'It's about saving lives, even if abstinence isn't the immediate goal.'*

Amira: *'We can combine harm reduction with pathways to treatment when someone's ready.'*

Science Break

Harm reduction strategies reduce the health and social consequences of substance use without requiring abstinence (Hawk et al., 2017). Evidence supports the effectiveness of MOUD, syringe service programs, and overdose prevention training in reducing mortality and improving health outcomes (Larochelle et al., 2018).

Key program components:

- Low-barrier access to services.
- MOUD and other evidence-based treatments.
- Overdose prevention education and naloxone distribution.
- Peer support and lived-experience staff.
- Integration with housing, medical, and mental health services.

Build It: Step-by-Step

1. Adopt a harm reduction philosophy in policies and training.
2. Provide low-barrier access to MOUD.
3. Implement syringe service programs and safe supply initiatives.
4. Train staff and participants in overdose prevention.
5. Offer pathways to treatment when individuals are ready.
6. Track health and engagement outcomes.

Practice Lab

- **Reflection**: How does your program currently approach substance use?
- **Prompt**: What harm reduction strategies could be implemented immediately?
- **Exercise**: Design a harm reduction plan for your setting.
- **Application**: Pilot one new harm reduction strategy and evaluate its impact.

4-Layer Integration

1. **Conscious**: Harm reduction policies and resource lists.
2. **Pre-conscious**: Visible availability of supplies and resources.
3. **Unconscious**: Addressing stigma among staff and participants.
4. **Existential**: Affirming worth and dignity regardless of substance use status.

References

- Hawk, M., Coulter, R. W. S., Egan, J. E., Fisk, S., Friedman, M. R., Tula, M., & Kinsky, S. (2017). Harm reduction principles for healthcare settings. *Harm Reduction Journal, 14*(1), 70.
- Larochelle, M. R., Bernson, D., Land, T., Stopka, T. J., Wang, N., Xuan, Z., Bagley, S. M., Liebschutz, J. M., & Walley, A. Y. (2018). Medication for opioid use disorder after nonfatal opioid overdose and association with mortality. *Annals of Internal Medicine, 169*(3), 137–145.

Chapter 23: Medical-Behavioral Integration

Ms. Chen, a 56-year-old woman with diabetes and depression, often missed her medical appointments. When a behavioral health specialist joined her primary care team, she began receiving mental health support during her routine check-ups. This integration helped her improve her blood sugar control and reduce depressive symptoms.

Conversation

Karen: *'Integrating medical and behavioral health care means better outcomes for both.'*

Mardoche: *'And it reduces the stigma of seeking mental health services.'*

Luis: *'It also makes it easier for patients to follow through when everything is in one place.'*

Amira: *'Plus, providers can coordinate in real-time instead of playing phone tag.'*

Science Break

Integrated care models improve access, quality, and efficiency of services for people with co-occurring medical and behavioral conditions (Butler et al., 2008). The Collaborative Care Model, for example, has been shown to improve depression and anxiety outcomes in primary care settings (Archer et al., 2012).

Key elements of successful integration:

- Co-location of services.
- Shared care plans and records.
- Regular case reviews.
- Use of care managers or coordinators.
- Measurement-based care.

Build It: Step-by-Step

1. Assess readiness for integration in both medical and behavioral teams.
2. Establish shared workflows and communication channels.
3. Train staff in collaborative care principles.
4. Implement shared electronic health records.
5. Monitor clinical and operational outcomes.
6. Adjust based on feedback from patients and staff.

Practice Lab

- **Reflection**: How well do your current services integrate medical and behavioral health?
- **Prompt**: What is one immediate step you could take toward integration?
- **Exercise**: Map a patient journey through integrated care.
- **Application**: Pilot a joint medical-behavioral visit and evaluate its effectiveness.

4-Layer Integration

1. **Conscious**: Shared care plans and co-location.
2. **Pre-conscious**: Warm handoffs between providers.
3. **Unconscious**: Breaking down silos between medical and behavioral staff.
4. **Existential**: Fostering a holistic view of health and well-being.

References

- Archer, J., Bower, P., Gilbody, S., Lovell, K., Richards, D., Gask, L., Dickens, C., & Coventry, P. (2012). Collaborative care for depression and anxiety problems. *Cochrane Database of Systematic Reviews, 2012*(10), CD006525.
- Butler, M., Kane, R. L., McAlpine, D., Kathol, R. G., Fu, S. S., Hagedorn, H., & Wilt, T. J. (2008). *Integration of mental health/substance abuse and primary care* (Evidence Report/Technology Assessment No. 173). Agency for Healthcare Research and Quality.

Chapter 24: Social Determinants of Health: Designing Upstream Interventions

James, a 47-year-old man with hypertension, often missed his medical appointments because he couldn't afford bus fare. When a community health program introduced a 'two quick wins' rule—addressing at least one social determinant and one clinical need within the first two weeks—James received a bus pass and had his blood pressure checked the same day. He began attending appointments regularly and saw improvements in his health.

Conversation

Karen: *'If we don't address social determinants, our clinical interventions won't stick.'*

Mardoche: *'Exactly. Housing, food, transportation, and income all influence health outcomes.'*

Luis: *'And sometimes the smallest changes, like a bus pass, can have the biggest impact.'*

Amira: *'That's why we track SDOH needs from day one.'*

Science Break

Social determinants of health (SDOH), the conditions in which people are born, grow, live, work, and age—account for up to 50% of health outcomes (Marmot & Wilkinson, 2005). Addressing SDOH through integrated services improves health equity, reduces costs, and increases engagement in care (Artiga & Hinton, 2018).

Key domains include:

- Economic stability.
- Education access and quality.
- Health care access and quality.
- Neighborhood and built environment.
- Social and community context.

Build It: Step-by-Step

1. Screen for SDOH needs at intake.
2. Prioritize 'two quick wins'—one social, one clinical.
3. Develop partnerships with community organizations.
4. Incorporate SDOH goals into care plans.
5. Track and evaluate SDOH interventions alongside clinical outcomes.

Practice Lab

- **Reflection**: Which SDOH factors most impact your population?
- **Prompt**: Which community partnerships could help address these factors?
- **Exercise**: Create an SDOH resource map for your program.
- **Application**: Implement the 'two quick wins' approach with five participants and track results.

4-Layer Integration

1. **Conscious**: SDOH screening tools and referral lists.
2. **Pre-conscious**: Automatic prompts to address SDOH early.
3. **Unconscious**: Recognizing and addressing biases about poverty and need.
4. **Existential**: Affirming that meeting basic needs is foundational to dignity and health.

References

- Artiga, S., & Hinton, E. (2018). Beyond health care: The role of social determinants in promoting health and health equity. Kaiser Family Foundation.
- Marmot, M., & Wilkinson, R. G. (Eds.). (2005). Social determinants of health (2nd ed.). Oxford University Press.

Part IV — Leading, Funding, and Protecting the Work

Chapter 25: Building the Right Team for the Work

When Amira was tasked with launching a new housing support program, she knew the right staff could make or break it. Instead of rushing to fill positions, she worked with HR to define roles clearly, sought candidates with both technical skills and empathy, and involved peers in the interview process. The result was a cohesive team that shared a common vision and worked seamlessly together.

Conversation

Karen: *'Hiring is one of the most important steps in program success.'*

Mardoche: *'We need people who can do the work and believe in the mission.'*

Luis: *'And keeping them means investing in their growth.'*

Amira: *'A strong team culture is built on trust, support, and accountability.'*

Science Break

Team effectiveness in social services is linked to clear role definitions, diversity, psychological safety, and ongoing professional development (Edmondson, 1999; Salas et al., 2008). High-functioning teams demonstrate better client outcomes, higher staff satisfaction, and lower turnover.

Key strategies for building effective teams:

- Clear job descriptions and expectations.
- Inclusive and equitable hiring practices.
- Comprehensive onboarding.
- Regular training and skill development.
- Team-building and reflective practice.

Build It: Step-by-Step

Step 1: Define roles and responsibilities for each position.
Step 2: Use behavioral interview questions to assess fit.
Step 3: Provide structured onboarding with mentoring.
Step 4: Establish clear communication channels.
Step 5: Schedule regular team check-ins and learning sessions.

Practice Lab

- **Reflection**: What qualities make someone successful in your program?
- **Prompt**: How can your hiring process better assess these qualities?
- **Exercise**: Draft an interview guide that incorporates values-based questions.
- **Application**: Plan your next team meeting to include a reflective practice segment.

4-Layer Integration

1. **Conscious**: Written role descriptions and onboarding checklists.
2. **Pre-conscious**: Cultural cues that reinforce collaboration.
3. **Unconscious**: Addressing team dynamics and unspoken norms.
4. **Existential**: Fostering a shared sense of purpose and belonging.

References

- Edmondson, A. (1999). Psychological safety and learning behavior in work teams. *Administrative Science Quarterly, 44*(2), 350–383.
- Salas, E., Wilson, K. A., Burke, C. S., & Wightman, D. C. (2008). Does crew resource management training work? An update, an extension, and some critical needs. *Human Factors, 48*(2), 392–412.

Chapter 26: Training, Supervision & Fidelity Support

Luis had been a case manager for only three weeks when he encountered his first crisis call from a client experiencing suicidal thoughts. Thanks to the crisis response training he received during onboarding and regular supervision from his team lead, he was able to respond calmly, engage the client, and connect them with immediate help. The situation reinforced the value of structured training and consistent supervision in preparing staff for high-stakes situations.

Conversation

Karen: *'Training isn't a one-time event. It's a continuous process.'*

Mardoche: *'And supervision is where we integrate learning into practice.'*

Luis: *'I felt prepared because I knew my supervisor would back me up.'*

Amira: *'When we invest in people's growth, we invest in the program's success.'*

Science Break

Effective training and supervision improve staff competence, confidence, and retention (Borders & Brown, 2005; Milne & James, 2002). Supervision models such as reflective supervision enhance critical thinking, self-awareness, and resilience among social service professionals.

Key elements of effective training and supervision:

- Competency-based training.
- Ongoing coaching and feedback.
- Opportunities for reflective practice.
- Structured supervision schedules.
- Use of outcome data to guide training priorities.

Build It: Step-by-Step

Step 1: Identify core competencies for each role.
Step 2: Develop an onboarding training plan.
Step 3: Implement a supervision framework (e.g., reflective supervision).
Step 4: Schedule regular supervision and coaching sessions.
Step 5: Evaluate training effectiveness through staff feedback and performance metrics.

Practice Lab

- **Reflection**: How consistent is supervision in your program?
- **Prompt**: Which training topics should be prioritized for your team?
- **Exercise**: Draft a supervision agenda template.
- **Application**: Implement a monthly reflective practice meeting for all staff.

4-Layer Integration

1. **Conscious**: Training manuals and supervision schedules.
2. **Pre-conscious**: Encouraging a growth mindset through feedback.
3. **Unconscious**: Shaping professional identity through mentorship.
4. **Existential**: Reinforcing purpose and meaning in daily work.

References

- Borders, L. D., & Brown, L. L. (2005). *The new handbook of counseling supervision*. Lawrence Erlbaum Associates.
- Milne, D., & James, I. A. (2002). The observed impact of training on competence in clinical supervision. *British Journal of Clinical Psychology, 41*(1), 55–72.

Chapter 27: Monitoring, Evaluation & Real-Time Learning

When the Midtown Youth Program launched, they had passion and energy, but no clear way to measure success. Three months in, the team introduced a simple monitoring and evaluation framework: tracking attendance, engagement, and progress on individualized goals. Within weeks, they identified which activities generated the highest participation and which needed rethinking. This allowed them to adapt quickly, leading to measurable improvements in both engagement and outcomes.

Conversation

Karen: *'If we don't measure it, we can't improve it.'*

Mardoche: *'And if we don't share results, we can't build trust with stakeholders.'*

Luis: *'Evaluation isn't just about proving success. It's about learning and adjusting.'*

Amira: *'And making sure we're actually delivering on what we promise.'*

Science Break

Monitoring and evaluation (M&E) provide data for decision-making, accountability, and program improvement (Patton, 2011). Effective M&E systems combine process evaluation (how the program is implemented) with outcome evaluation (results achieved). Mixed-method approaches, combining quantitative data with qualitative insights, offer a fuller picture of program impact.

Core components of an effective M&E system:

- Clear goals and indicators.
- Baseline data collection.
- Regular monitoring.
- Data analysis and interpretation.
- Feedback loops for continuous improvement.

Build It: Step-by-Step

Step 1: Define program goals and measurable indicators.
Step 2: Collect baseline data before implementation.
Step 3: Establish a monitoring schedule and assign responsibilities.
Step 4: Analyze data regularly and compare against goals.
Step 5: Use findings to adapt and strengthen the program.

Practice Lab

- **Reflection**: How well are you currently measuring program success?
- **Prompt**: What additional indicators could give you a better understanding of your impact?
- **Exercise**: Create a basic M&E plan for a program you manage.
- **Application**: Implement one new feedback mechanism for participants and staff.

4-Layer Integration

1. **Conscious**: Data collection tools and indicator lists.
2. **Pre-conscious**: Regular review habits that make M&E routine.
3. **Unconscious**: Valuing learning over perfection.
4. **Existential**: Ensuring that what we measure aligns with what truly matters to participants and the community.

References

Patton, M. Q. (2011). *Developmental evaluation: Applying complexity concepts to enhance innovation and use*. Guilford Press.

Chapter 28: The Psychology of Teams — Burnout, Resistance, and Buy-In

The program looked perfect on paper, yet failed in practice. Staff appeared resistant, but beneath it was burnout, overwhelm, and lack of trust. When leadership shifted focus from the program to the team, everything changed. The issue was not design; rather, it was the psychology of the people implementing it.

Conversation

Karen: *"Resistance is information."*

Mardoche: *"Burnout is misalignment between effort and meaning."*

Amira: *"Buy-in is alignment, not agreement."*

Science Break

Burnout, resistance, and buy-in are interconnected. Burnout reflects exhaustion and misalignment; while resistance reflects perceived threat and uncertainty. Buy-in emerges when autonomy, competence, and relatedness are met (Deci & Ryan, 2000).

Build It: Step-by-Step

1. Diagnose the team.
2. Name what is happening.
3. Reduce complexity.
4. Create early wins.
5. Build psychological safety.
6. Involve the team.
7. Reinforce meaning.
8. Monitor burnout.

Practice Lab

- **Reflection**: Where is your team?
- **Prompt**: What is unspoken?
- **Exercise**: Create a team check-in.

- **Application**: Hold one listening session.

4-Layer Integration

1. **Conscious**: Structure.
2. **Pre-conscious**: Habits.
3. **Unconscious**: Fear/resistance.
4. **Existential**: Purpose.

References

- Deci, E. L., & Ryan, R. M. (2000). Self-determination theory and the facilitation of intrinsic motivation, social development, and well-being. *American Psychologist, 55*(1), 68–78.
- Edmondson, A. (1999). Psychological safety and learning behavior in work teams. *Administrative Science Quarterly, 44*(2), 350–383.
- Maslach, C., & Jackson, S. E. (1981). The measurement of experienced burnout. *Journal of Occupational Behavior, 2*(2), 99–113.

Chapter 29: Sustainability Planning (Before, During, and After Funding)

The Community Wellness Hub had just completed its first year, with glowing feedback from participants and partners. But as the initial grant funding neared its end, the team realized they had no sustainability plan in place. They scrambled to secure new funding, strengthen partnerships, and diversify revenue streams. By the following year, they had created a long-term sustainability strategy, ensuring the Hub's future for years to come.

Conversation

Karen: *'We often think about launching programs but not sustaining them.'*

Mardoche: *'Sustainability planning should start before the program begins.'*

Luis: *'Diversifying funding is essential, but so is building community ownership.'*

Amira: *'A sustainable program is one that can adapt and survive in changing conditions.'*

Science Break

Sustainability in social services involves securing the resources, community support, and organizational capacity to maintain program benefits over time (Scheirer, 2005). Research shows that programs with diversified funding, strong leadership, and integrated community partnerships are more likely to survive beyond initial funding cycles.

Key components of sustainability planning:

- Early integration of sustainability goals.
- Funding diversification (grants, donations, earned income).
- Strong stakeholder and community engagement.
- Clear succession planning.
- Continuous program evaluation and adaptation.

Build It: Step-by-Step

Step 1: Identify long-term goals for the program.
Step 2: Map potential funding sources and revenue streams.
Step 3: Build strong relationships with stakeholders.
Step 4: Develop a plan for leadership succession.
Step 5: Incorporate adaptability into program design.

Practice Lab

- **Reflection**: How early in your program cycle do you start planning for sustainability?
- **Prompt**: What partnerships could strengthen your long-term success?
- **Exercise**: Draft a basic sustainability plan for your program.
- **Application**: Identify one new potential funding source and take the first step toward engaging it.

4-Layer Integration

1. **Conscious**: Written sustainability plan and funding calendar.
2. **Pre-conscious**: Regularly tracking funding and partnership opportunities.
3. **Unconscious**: Embedding resilience into organizational culture.
4. **Existential**: Aligning sustainability with the mission's deeper purpose.

References

Scheirer, M. A. (2005). Is sustainability possible? A review and commentary on empirical studies of program sustainability. *American Journal of Evaluation, 26*(3), 320–347.

Chapter 30: Funding Models That Work — Billing, Grants, Value-Based Care, and Hybrid Models

The program was working until the funding ended. Engagement improved, crises dropped, and staff aligned. Then came the question: "How is this funded?" Without a sustainable model, the program slowed and stopped. It did not stop because it failed; rather, because it wasn't funded to work.

Conversation

Karen: *"Programs don't die because they fail. They die because they're not funded."*

Mardoche: *"Funding is the oxygen."*

Luis: *"So design and funding must happen together."*

Science Break

Sustainable programs align services with funding. Systems are shifting from volume-based to value-based care, rewarding outcomes and efficiency; and misalignment leads to collapse; while alignment enables scale.

Build It: Step-by-Step

1. Start with funding early.
2. Understand four streams (billing, grants, value-based, hybrid).
3. Match activities to funding.
4. Design for billability.
5. Use grants to launch, not sustain.
6. Track outcomes for value-based alignment.
7. Build a sustainability plan.
8. Speak funder language (cost, outcomes, efficiency).

Practice Lab

- **Reflection**: What is unfunded?
- **Prompt**: What survives without current funding?
- **Exercise**: Create a funding map.
- **Application**: Identify one billable activity and one outcome metric.

4-Layer Integration

1. **Conscious**: Billing, budgets.
2. **Pre-conscious**: Documentation habits.
3. **Unconscious**: Beliefs about money.
4. **Existential**: Sustainability as responsibility.

References

- Berwick, D. M., Nolan, T. W., & Whittington, J. (2008). The triple aim: Care, health, and cost. *Health Affairs, 27*(3), 759–769.
- Centers for Medicare & Medicaid Services. (n.d.). *Value-based care*. U.S. Department of Health & Human Services.
- Nuffield Trust. (2011). *Where next for integrated care organisations in the English NHS?* Nuffield Trust.
- Porter, M. E., & Teisberg, E. O. (2006). *Redefining health care: Creating value-based competition on results*. Harvard Business School Press.

Chapter 31: Scaling & Replication: Protect the Core, Adapt the Rest

When the Bridge to College program in one city showed dramatic success in increasing enrollment for first-generation students, the team received requests from other communities to replicate it. Instead of simply copying and pasting the model, they conducted a readiness assessment, adapted materials to local contexts, and trained new teams to deliver the program effectively. This thoughtful approach ensured that the program's core values remained intact while meeting the unique needs of each site.

Conversation

Karen: *'Scaling is not just doing more of the same. It's doing it right in more places.'*

Mardoche: *'We have to protect the core model while adapting to new contexts.'*

Luis: *'Replication without adaptation can set programs up for failure.'*

Amira: *'Scaling is as much about capacity as it is about demand.'*

Science Break

Scaling and replication require balancing fidelity to the original model with flexibility to local needs (Fixsen et al., 2005). Implementation science emphasizes the importance of pilot testing, stakeholder engagement, and infrastructure readiness before expansion. Well-planned scaling leads to broader impact, while poorly planned replication risks diluting effectiveness.

Core principles for scaling and replication:

- Maintain core program components (fidelity).
- Assess local capacity and readiness.
- Adapt non-core elements for cultural and contextual fit.
- Provide thorough training and technical assistance.
- Monitor outcomes to ensure quality across sites.

Build It: Step-by-Step

Step 1: Identify the program's core components that must remain unchanged.
Step 2: Conduct readiness assessments in potential expansion sites.
Step 3: Adapt materials and processes for local relevance.
Step 4: Train new teams and provide ongoing technical assistance.
Step 5: Monitor performance and adjust as needed.

Practice Lab

- **Reflection**: What aspects of your program are non-negotiable for maintaining quality?
- **Prompt**: What would need to change to make your program successful in a different community?
- **Exercise**: Draft a scaling plan that includes fidelity and adaptation strategies.
- **Application**: Identify one potential new site and conduct a preliminary readiness assessment.

4-Layer Integration

1. **Conscious**: Written scaling plan and fidelity checklist.
2. **Pre-conscious**: Cultivating flexibility and openness to feedback.
3. **Unconscious**: Recognizing and addressing assumptions about 'what works' everywhere.
4. **Existential**: Expanding reach without losing the heart of the mission.

References

Fixsen, D. L., Naoom, S. F., Blase, K. A., Friedman, R. M., & Wallace, F. (2005). *Implementation research: A synthesis of the literature*. University of South Florida, Louis de la Parte Florida Mental Health Institute.

Chapter 32: Policy, Advocacy & System Influence

The Safe Streets Initiative had been working tirelessly to reduce youth violence in their neighborhood. While their local program had seen some success, they realized that without policy changes, such as improved access to mental health services and adjustments to policing strategies, their impact would be limited. By forming coalitions, presenting data to policymakers, and engaging in community advocacy, they influenced legislation that supported broader systemic change, amplifying the reach of their work.

Conversation

Karen: *'Policy work isn't optional if we want long-term change.'*

Mardoche: *'Advocacy gives our programs a voice in shaping the environment we operate in.'*

Luis: *'Sometimes, the most impactful thing we can do is change the rules of the game.'*

Amira: *'And the people closest to the problem need to be at the table for solutions.'*

Science Break

Integrating policy and advocacy into program work enhances sustainability and systemic impact (Baum et al., 2006). Policy change can address structural barriers that limit program effectiveness. Advocacy strategies range from grassroots mobilization to legislative lobbying, and from public education campaigns to coalition building.

Key elements of effective policy and advocacy integration:

- Align advocacy goals with program mission.
- Use data and stories to influence decision-makers.
- Build partnerships with advocacy organizations.
- Engage directly with affected communities.

- Monitor policy changes and adapt program strategies accordingly.

Build It: Step-by-Step

Step 1: Identify policy barriers affecting your program's goals.
Step 2: Develop an advocacy strategy that aligns with your mission.
Step 3: Gather and present evidence to support your policy recommendations.
Step 4: Build coalitions with aligned organizations.
Step 5: Monitor policy developments and adjust your approach as needed.

Practice Lab

- **Reflection**: What policy barriers most affect your work right now?
- **Prompt**: Which policymakers or community leaders could be allies for your cause?
- **Exercise**: Draft a short policy brief related to your program area.
- **Application**: Attend or organize a meeting with policymakers to discuss your recommendations.

4-Layer Integration

1. **Conscious**: Written advocacy plan and policy priority list.
2. **Pre-conscious**: Building habits of scanning for policy opportunities.
3. **Unconscious**: Recognizing how systemic factors influence day-to-day program work.
4. **Existential**: Connecting program goals to the broader pursuit of justice and equity.

References

Baum, F., Lawless, A., & Delany, T. (2006). Health promotion and policy: Partnerships in action. *Health Promotion Journal of Australia, 17*(3), 240–246.

Chapter 33: Becoming a Learning Organization

At Hopewell Services, a staff meeting once meant endless updates and little reflection. But after adopting a learning organization approach, every meeting included data reviews, case discussions, and time for sharing lessons learned. Over time, this shift led to innovative solutions, improved morale, and better client outcomes. Staff began to see challenges as opportunities for growth, not setbacks.

Conversation

Karen: *'A learning organization is like a living organism. It adapts and grows.'*

Mardoche: *'It's about embedding continuous improvement into the culture.'*

Luis: *'Data without reflection is just numbers. Reflection turns it into knowledge.'*

Amira: *'And knowledge is only powerful if we act on it.'*

Science Break

A learning organization is one that continuously transforms itself by facilitating the learning of its members and continuously being adaptive to its environment (Senge, 1990). Research highlights the importance of feedback loops, psychological safety, and shared leadership in fostering learning cultures.

Key features of a learning organization:

- Shared vision and collective purpose.
- Systems thinking to understand complex relationships.
- Encouragement of team learning and dialogue.
- Structures for capturing and sharing knowledge.
- Continuous experimentation and innovation.

Build It: Step-by-Step

Step 1: Establish a shared vision for continuous improvement.
Step 2: Create regular spaces for reflection and dialogue.
Step 3: Implement systems for capturing and sharing lessons learned.
Step 4: Encourage experimentation and safe risk-taking.
Step 5: Measure and celebrate progress over time.

Practice Lab

- **Reflection**: How often do your teams reflect on successes and failures?
- **Prompt**: What structures could you put in place to encourage organizational learning?
- **Exercise**: Map your organization's current feedback loops.
- **Application**: Pilot one change to increase learning and measure its impact.

4-Layer Integration

1. **Conscious**: Written policies for reflection, learning, and innovation.
2. **Pre-conscious**: Regularly capturing lessons learned in daily work.
3. **Unconscious**: Cultivating curiosity and openness to change.
4. **Existential**: Seeing learning as part of the deeper purpose of serving others.

References

Senge, P. M. (1990). *The fifth discipline: The art and practice of the learning organization*. Doubleday/Currency.

Chapter 34: Crisis-Resilient Program Design (Readiness, Response & Recovery)

When the Community Wellness Hub launched, it was powered by passion, a small grant, and volunteer energy. The first year was electric, full of ideas and rapid implementation. But as the grant ended, the team faced a stark reality: without a sustainability plan, the program could collapse. By diversifying funding streams, building partnerships, and embedding services into existing institutions, they not only survived but thrived for over a decade.

Conversation

Karen: *'Sustainability starts on day one, not when the money runs out.'*

Mardoche: *'Too many great programs disappear because they don't think ahead.'*

Luis: *'We need to think about funding, leadership, and community ownership.'*

Amira: *'And adaptability—the ability to evolve keeps programs relevant.'*

Science Break

Program sustainability refers to the capacity to maintain program services over time while continuing to produce benefits for the target population (Scheirer, 2005). Research indicates that sustainability depends on multiple factors: diversified funding, strong leadership, integration with community structures, ongoing evaluation, and the ability to adapt to changing needs.

Core sustainability strategies:

- Develop multiple funding streams (grants, donations, earned income).
- Build strong partnerships and community buy-in.
- Institutionalize key components within established organizations.

- Monitor performance and adapt to maintain relevance.
- Invest in leadership development and succession planning.

Build It: Step-by-Step

Step 1: Identify and document core program components.
Step 2: Develop a diversified funding strategy.
Step 3: Strengthen partnerships and engage the community.
Step 4: Integrate services into stable institutions where possible.
Step 5: Establish a system for ongoing evaluation and adaptation.

Practice Lab

- **Reflection**: What is your program's current sustainability risk?
- **Prompt**: Which potential partners could help embed your services more deeply in the community?
- **Exercise**: Draft a one-page sustainability plan.
- **Application**: Identify one new funding source to pursue within the next quarter.

4-Layer Integration

1. **Conscious**: Written sustainability plan and funding strategy.
2. **Pre-conscious**: Cultivating habits of looking ahead for long-term stability.
3. **Unconscious**: Recognizing the tendency to focus on short-term wins over lasting impact.
4. **Existential**: Committing to the program's deeper mission beyond immediate challenges.

References

Scheirer, M. A. (2005). Is sustainability possible? A review and commentary on empirical studies of program sustainability. *American Journal of Evaluation, 26*(3), 320–347.

Part V — Evaluation, CQI, Equity & Large-Scale Impact

Chapter 35: Measuring Long-Term Impact Without Complexity

The Early Start Literacy Program celebrated its fifth anniversary with an alumni gathering. Teachers, parents, and former students shared stories of how early literacy support changed educational trajectories. Beyond improved reading scores, students reported higher self-esteem, greater school engagement, and broader life opportunities. By tracking these outcomes over years, the program demonstrated not only short-term success but lasting generational impact.

Conversation

Karen: *'We often measure what's easy, not what's meaningful.'*

Mardoche: *'Long-term impact takes patience. It doesn't show up on a quarterly report.'*

Luis: *'We have to follow people's journeys, not just their snapshots.'*

Amira: *'And sometimes the biggest impact is invisible until years later.'*

Science Break

Measuring long-term impact involves assessing sustained changes in knowledge, behavior, health, or well-being that occur as a result of a program (Rossi et al., 2019). This requires longitudinal data collection, mixed-method approaches, and an understanding of contextual factors that influence outcomes.

Best practices for measuring long-term impact:

- Define clear, long-term indicators linked to program goals.
- Use both quantitative and qualitative measures.
- Implement longitudinal tracking systems.
- Control for external influences where possible.
- Share findings with stakeholders to reinforce support and funding.

Build It: Step-by-Step

Step 1: Identify desired long-term outcomes during program design.
Step 2: Develop indicators and measurement tools for these outcomes.
Step 3: Establish a system for longitudinal data collection.
Step 4: Analyze trends and contextual influences.
Step 5: Use results for continuous improvement and advocacy.

Practice Lab

- **Reflection:** What long-term outcomes would you like to track in your work?
- **Prompt:** How could you follow participants beyond program completion?
- **Exercise:** Draft a basic plan for longitudinal impact measurement.
- **Application:** Begin collecting at least one long-term indicator starting this year.

4-Layer Integration

1. **Conscious**: Clear list of long-term indicators.
2. **Pre-conscious**: Regular follow-up with past participants.
3. **Unconscious**: Valuing deep, lasting change over quick wins.
4. **Existential**: Connecting your work to future generations' opportunities.

References

Rossi, P. H., Lipsey, M. W., & Henry, G. T. (2019). *Evaluation: A systematic approach* (8th ed.). SAGE Publications.

Chapter 36: What Gets Measured Gets Done — Designing Metrics That Change Behavior

The team had data, and lots of it. They had dashboards, reports, and summaries. Yet nothing changed. When they shifted from asking *'What should we measure?'* to *'What behavior do we want to change?'*, everything shifted. They focused on a few key behaviors, and outcomes began to move.

Conversation

Karen: '*Measurement is about behavior.*'

Mardoche: '*If behavior isn't changing, your metrics aren't working.*'

Luis: *'So, clarity and actionability matter most.'*

Science Break

Metrics shape behavior through attention and feedback loops. Too many metrics reduce effectiveness. Simple, visible metrics outperform complex dashboards.

Build It: Step-by-Step

1. Start with behavior.
2. Limit to 3–5 metrics.
3. Make metrics visible.
4. Ensure actionability.
5. Create feedback loops.
6. Align with workflow.
7. Avoid overload.
8. Reinforce behavior.

Metrics Model

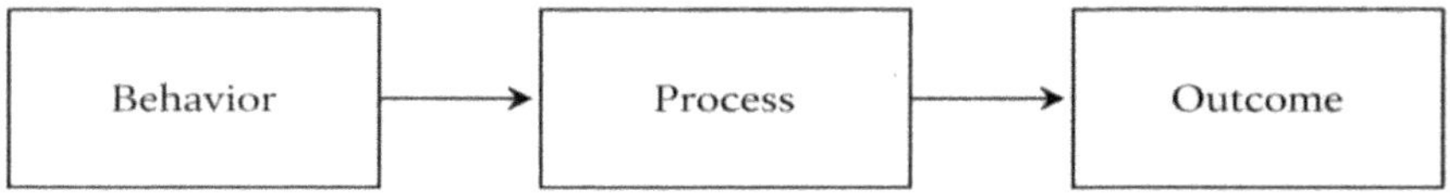

Practice Lab

- **Reflection**: What isn't changing behavior?
- **Prompt**: What are your top five metrics?
- **Exercise**: Redesign your metrics.
- **Application**: Remove two low-value metrics.

4-Layer Integration

1. **Conscious**: Dashboards.
2. **Pre-conscious**: Tracking habits.
3. **Unconscious**: Fear of measurement.
4. **Existential**: Accountability.

References

- Carver, C. S., & Scheier, M. F. (1982). Control theory: A useful conceptual framework for personality-social, clinical, and health psychology. *Psychological Bulletin, 92*(1), 111–135.
- Goodhart, C. A. E. (1975). Problems of monetary management: The U.K. experience. In *Papers in monetary economics* (Vol. 1, pp. 91–121). Reserve Bank of Australia.
- Kahneman, D. (2011). *Thinking, fast and slow*. Farrar, Straus and Giroux.
- Kerr, S. (1975). On the folly of rewarding A, while hoping for B. *Academy of Management Journal, 18*(4), 769–783.

Chapter 37: Scaling What Works (Advanced Models & Case Studies)

A small pilot program in a single urban neighborhood helped justice-involved youth find employment and housing. The results were striking. Recidivism dropped by 40%, and 75% of participants found stable jobs. When the city decided to replicate the program across multiple districts, leaders faced new challenges: adapting to different community needs, maintaining fidelity to the original model, and ensuring quality at scale. By balancing core principles with local flexibility, the program became a model for statewide reform.

Conversation

Karen: *'Scaling is not just doing more of the same. It's doing it in a way that works in new contexts.'*

Mardoche: *'You can lose the magic if you're not careful.'*

Luis: *'We have to know which parts are non-negotiable and which can be adapted.'*

Amira: *'And scaling requires resources, leadership, and a clear plan for quality control.'*

Science Break

Scaling a program involves expanding its reach to serve more people or new populations while maintaining or improving outcomes (Cooley & Kohl, 2006). Successful scaling requires identifying core components, building capacity, ensuring fidelity, and adapting to local contexts.

Key elements for scaling:

- Define the essential features of the program.
- Assess preparedness for scaling: organizational, financial, and political.
- Develop training and quality assurance systems.
- Create flexible implementation guides.

- Monitor and evaluate outcomes during and after scale-up.

Build It: Step-by-Step

Step 1: Identify and document core program elements.
Step 2: Assess readiness and capacity for scale-up.
Step 3: Develop a detailed scaling plan.
Step 4: Train staff and partners for fidelity and adaptation.
Step 5: Monitor quality and outcomes during scale-up.
Step 6: Adjust based on ongoing feedback.

Practice Lab

- **Reflection**: Which aspects of your program are essential to its success?
- **Prompt**: What would scaling look like in your context?
- **Exercise**: Map potential new locations or populations for expansion.
- **Application**: Draft a scaling readiness checklist for your program.

4-Layer Integration

1. **Conscious**: Written scaling plan with clear steps and measures.
2. **Pre-conscious**: Building habits of documenting and codifying best practices.
3. **Unconscious**: Recognizing fears of losing control and addressing them.
4. **Existential**: Committing to impact at a larger scale without losing mission integrity.

References

Cooley, L., & Kohl, R. (2006). *Scaling up—From vision to large-scale change: A management framework for practitioners*. Management Systems International.

Chapter 38: Designing for Equity (Access, Experience & Outcomes)

When the River City Health Collaborative reviewed its patient data, they discovered glaring disparities in health outcomes between neighborhoods. Clients in predominantly Black and Latino areas faced higher rates of preventable illness, longer wait times, and lower treatment completion rates. The program's leadership realized that without intentionally addressing equity from the start, well-meaning interventions could unintentionally reinforce existing disparities. They redesigned services with community voices at the center, leading to measurable improvements in access and outcomes.

Conversation

Karen: *'Equity isn't just a nice-to-have. It's fundamental to effective care.'*

Mardoche: *'If we ignore structural inequities, our programs risk perpetuating harm.'*

Luis: *'Equity has to be designed into every layer, from outreach to evaluation.'*

Amira: *'And that means sharing power, not just inviting people to the table.'*

Science Break

Equity in program design ensures that all individuals have fair and just opportunities to achieve optimal outcomes (Braveman & Gruskin, 2003). This involves recognizing and addressing systemic barriers, power imbalances, and historical injustices. Research shows that equity-focused programs lead to better population-level outcomes and reduce disparities across health, education, and social services.

Core strategies for embedding equity:

- Conduct equity impact assessments before launch.

- Engage affected communities in co-design and decision-making.
- Collect and analyze disaggregated data.
- Address barriers related to language, culture, transportation, and access.
- Ensure accountability through equity performance metrics.

Build It: Step-by-Step

Step 1: Define equity in the context of your program.
Step 2: Engage diverse stakeholders from the earliest planning stages.
Step 3: Identify and address systemic barriers.
Step 4: Collect and review equity-focused data regularly.
Step 5: Adjust strategies based on findings.
Step 6: Hold the program accountable to equity goals.

Practice Lab

- **Reflection**: Where might inequities exist in your current or planned program?
- **Prompt**: Who is not at the table but should be?
- **Exercise**: Conduct an equity gap analysis for your program.
- **Application**: Implement one change this quarter to address an identified inequity.

4-Layer Integration

1. **Conscious**: Written equity strategy with measurable goals.
2. **Pre-conscious**: Habits of questioning who benefits and who is left out.
3. **Unconscious**: Recognizing implicit biases and systemic blind spots.
4. **Existential**: Committing to justice as a core purpose of the work.

References

Braveman, P., & Gruskin, S. (2003). Defining equity in health. *Journal of Epidemiology & Community Health, 57*(4), 254–258.

Chapter 39: Ethical Program Design — Power, Equity, and Responsibility in Systems

The program was efficient and outcomes looked strong until patterns revealed inequities. Language barriers, cultural mismatches, and structural assumptions led to unequal outcomes. The realization: harm wasn't intended, but it wasn't prevented either.

Conversation

Karen: '*Ethics is about design'*.

Mardoche: '*Systems create predictable outcomes.'*

Luis: '*So, fairness must be built in.'*

Amira: '*Otherwise, inequity becomes systemic.'*

Science Break

Ethical program design integrates autonomy, beneficence, nonmaleficence, and justice. Structural inequities often arise unintentionally but persist without measurement and redesign.

Build It: Step-by-Step

1. Map power in the system.
2. Identify who benefits and who doesn't.
3. Design for equity (not equality).
4. Build participant feedback loops.
5. Anticipate unintended consequences.
6. Measure equity.
7. Create accountability.
8. Align ethics with daily practice.

Practice Lab

- **Reflection**: Who is not benefiting?
- **Prompt**: Where is unintended harm?
- **Exercise**: Conduct an equity audit.

- **Application**: Implement one structural change.

4-Layer Integration

1. **Conscious**: Policies and metrics.
2. **Pre-conscious**: Habits and workflows.
3. **Unconscious**: Bias and blind spots.
4. **Existential**: Dignity and justice.

References

- Bailey, Z. D., Krieger, N., Agénor, M., Graves, J., Linos, N., & Bassett, M. T. (2017). Structural racism and health inequities in the USA: Evidence and interventions. *The Lancet, 389*(10077), 1453–1463.
- Beauchamp, T. L., & Childress, J. F. (2001). *Principles of biomedical ethics* (5th ed.). Oxford University Press.
- Braveman, P. (2014). What are health disparities and health equity? We need to be clear. *Public Health Reports, 129*(Suppl. 2), 5–8.
- Farmer, P. (2004). An anthropology of structural violence. *Current Anthropology, 45*(3), 305–325.

Chapter 40: Sustaining Momentum Over Time

Five years after launching the Community Wellness Initiative, participation rates had plateaued. Initial enthusiasm from staff, partners, and clients had faded. Some programs had drifted from their original purpose, and newer staff were less connected to the founding vision. Leadership recognized that sustaining momentum required intentional strategies to re-energize stakeholders, celebrate progress, and adapt to evolving needs. Through renewed community engagement, refreshed training, and visible leadership commitment, the initiative regained its energy and continued to expand its impact.

Conversation

Karen: *'It's not enough to launch well. You have to sustain over the long haul.'*

Mardoche: *'Momentum fades if we don't invest in keeping people connected to the mission.'*

Luis: *'We have to regularly remind ourselves why this work matters.'*

Amira: *'And we need to evolve while staying true to our core values.'*

Science Break

Program sustainability is the capacity to maintain services, benefits, and impact over time (Scheirer & Dearing, 2011). Sustaining momentum involves financial stability, ongoing stakeholder engagement, staff retention, and adaptability to changing circumstances.

Evidence-based strategies to sustain momentum:

- Regularly communicate progress and success stories.
- Provide ongoing training and professional development.
- Build diversified funding streams.

- Foster a strong organizational culture.
- Monitor and adapt to changes in community needs and policy environments.

Build It: Step-by-Step

Step 1: Create a sustainability plan during program design.
Step 2: Establish mechanisms for regular reflection and renewal.
Step 3: Maintain consistent communication with all stakeholders.
Step 4: Invest in staff development and leadership pipelines.
Step 5: Diversify funding and resources.
Step 6: Adapt program elements to remain relevant.

Practice Lab

- **Reflection**: Where has momentum waned in your current program?
- **Prompt**: What strategies could re-energize your team and stakeholders?
- **Exercise**: Identify one sustainability risk and create a mitigation plan.
- **Application**: Implement one visible renewal activity within the next month.

4-Layer Integration

1. **Conscious**: Written sustainability plan with timelines.
2. **Pre-conscious**: Regular recognition of achievements.
3. **Unconscious**: Resisting complacency by fostering curiosity.
4. **Existential**: Embracing the program's mission as a living, evolving commitment.

References

Scheirer, M. A., & Dearing, J. W. (2011). An agenda for research on the sustainability of public health programs. *American Journal of Public Health, 101*(11), 2059–2067.

Chapter 41: Building Programs for Crisis Readiness & Adaptability

During the peak of the COVID-19 pandemic, the Horizon Youth Center faced unprecedented challenges. In-person programs halted overnight, staff were redeployed, and community needs skyrocketed. Because the center had no formal crisis plan, the first few months were chaotic—reactive rather than proactive. Eventually, the leadership team developed a rapid response framework, including virtual program delivery, emergency communication channels, and partnerships for food and mental health services. When a severe winter storm hit two years later, they were ready, and their services never stopped.

Conversation

Karen: *'Crisis readiness is like insurance. You hope you never need it, but you're grateful when you do.'*

Mardoche: *'The question is not if a crisis will happen, but when.'*

Luis: *'We can design resilience into our programs from the start.'*

Amira: *'And readiness is about people as much as it is about procedures.'*

Science Break

Crisis readiness in program design refers to the ability to continue essential operations and services during and after a disruptive event (Kapucu & Van Wart, 2006). It involves proactive planning, flexible infrastructure, and trained staff who can respond quickly.

Key elements of crisis readiness:

- Risk assessment and scenario planning.
- Continuity of operations plans (COOP).
- Redundant systems for communication and data.
- Training and drills for staff.
- Partnerships for emergency resource sharing.

Build It: Step-by-Step

Step 1: Conduct a comprehensive risk and vulnerability assessment.
Step 2: Identify essential services and functions.
Step 3: Develop continuity and contingency plans.
Step 4: Establish clear crisis communication protocols.
Step 5: Train all staff in emergency procedures.
Step 6: Test and update the plan regularly.

Practice Lab

- **Reflection**: What types of crises are most likely to disrupt your program?
- **Prompt**: Which program functions must continue under any circumstances?
- **Exercise**: Draft a crisis communication flowchart.
- **Application**: Conduct a tabletop exercise simulating a crisis scenario.

4-Layer Integration

1. **Conscious**: Written crisis readiness plan with clear protocols.
2. **Pre-conscious**: Staff trained in emergency responses.
3. **Unconscious**: Confidence in the team's ability to respond under pressure.
4. **Existential**: Viewing readiness as an act of care for the community.

References

Kapucu, N., & Van Wart, M. (2006). The evolving role of the public sector in managing catastrophic disasters: Lessons learned. *Administration & Society, 38*(3), 279–308.

Chapter 42: Integrating Across Systems (Education, Housing, Justice, Health)

The Family Pathways Initiative began as a collaboration between a local mental health clinic and the school district. Over time, they added partnerships with the juvenile justice system, housing agencies, and primary care providers. This integration allowed families to navigate services seamlessly, reduced duplication, and improved outcomes. One family, previously juggling appointments at four different locations, could now access coordinated care through a single point of contact.

Conversation

Karen: *'Integration isn't just about working together. It's about thinking together.'*

Mardoche: *'Exactly. Otherwise, you just have parallel tracks that never meet.'*

Luis: *'Shared goals and communication are what make integration work.'*

Amira: *'And a willingness to let go of territorial thinking.'*

Science Break

Systems integration involves aligning policies, funding, services, and information systems to improve access, quality, and efficiency of care (Kodner & Spreeuwenberg, 2002). In mental health and social services, integration reduces fragmentation, supports holistic care, and improves client outcomes.

Principles of effective integration:

- Shared vision and objectives.
- Cross-sector leadership.
- Coordinated service delivery models.
- Integrated data systems.
- Continuous joint evaluation and quality improvement.

Build It: Step-by-Step

Step 1: Identify overlapping goals across systems.
Step 2: Build relationships with key leaders in each system.
Step 3: Develop a shared governance structure.
Step 4: Create protocols for information sharing and coordinated care.
Step 5: Pilot integrated service delivery in a focused area.
Step 6: Scale integration based on pilot results and feedback.

Practice Lab

- **Reflection**: Which systems intersect with your program's work?
- **Prompt**: What barriers currently exist between your program and other systems?
- **Exercise**: Map potential integration points across systems.
- **Application**: Initiate one cross-system partnership in the next quarter.

4-Layer Integration

1. **Conscious**: Documented integration plan with clear roles.
2. **Pre-conscious**: Regular cross-system meetings and updates.
3. **Unconscious**: Mindset of collaboration over competition.
4. **Existential**: Recognizing that integration serves the whole person, not just a program's goals.

References

Kodner, D. L., & Spreeuwenberg, C. (2002). Integrated care: Meaning, logic, applications, and implications—A discussion paper. *International Journal of Integrated Care, 2*, e12.

Chapter 43: Cross-Sector Partnerships That Transform Communities

When the Community Wellness Coalition launched, it brought together healthcare providers, schools, housing agencies, and local businesses. Initially, each sector had its own priorities and language, making collaboration slow and sometimes tense. Over time, through regular meetings, shared goals, and joint projects, they began to see the power of working together. One highlight: a coordinated outreach program that connected clients to medical care, job training, and stable housing—transforming lives in ways no single sector could have achieved alone.

Conversation

Karen: *'Partnership is about finding the overlap between missions.'*

Mardoche: *'And about learning to speak each other's language.'*

Luis: *'Trust doesn't happen overnight. It's built over time.'*

Amira: *'When sectors come together, the sum is greater than its parts.'*

Science Break

Cross-sector partnerships involve collaboration between organizations from different sectors (e.g., public health, education, housing, justice) to address complex social issues.

Research shows that successful partnerships share:

- A clear, shared purpose.
- Mutual trust and respect.
- Formal agreements and defined roles.
- Ongoing communication channels.
- Shared measurement systems.

The Collective Impact framework (Kania & Kramer, 2011) emphasizes the need for a common agenda, shared measurement, mutually reinforcing activities, continuous communication, and backbone support organizations.

Build It: Step-by-Step

Step 1: Identify potential partners with aligned missions.
Step 2: Establish a shared vision and goals.
Step 3: Define roles, responsibilities, and decision-making processes.
Step 4: Develop formal agreements (e.g., MOUs).
Step 5: Create shared metrics to track impact.
Step 6: Invest in relationship-building and regular communication.

Practice Lab

- **Reflection**: What sectors could strengthen your program's impact if you partnered with them?
- **Prompt**: What value could you offer a potential partner?
- **Exercise**: Map your community's key sectors and potential partner organizations.
- **Application**: Initiate one exploratory meeting with a new sector partner.

4-Layer Integration

1. **Conscious**: Written partnership plan.
2. **Pre-conscious**: Awareness of each partner's strengths and constraints.
3. **Unconscious**: Mindset of collaboration over competition.
4. **Existential**: Belief in the power of collective action to create systemic change.

References

Kania, J., & Kramer, M. (2011). Collective impact. *Stanford Social Innovation Review, 9*(1), 36–41.

Chapter 44: Leveraging Data for Continuous Improvement

At the Sunrise Recovery Center, staff collected client satisfaction surveys for years, but the data mostly sat in a filing cabinet. When a new director arrived, she transformed how the center used data, reviewing results monthly, discussing trends in team meetings, and making targeted changes based on the findings. Over time, client outcomes improved, staff morale increased, and funders took notice. The center's culture shifted from data as paperwork to data as a tool for transformation.

Conversation

Karen: *'Data is only valuable if you use it.'*

Mardoche: *'It's not about collecting more data. It's about collecting the right data.'*

Luis: *'And making sure the people on the ground actually see and understand it.'*

Amira: *'Data should tell a story that drives action.'*

Science Break

Continuous improvement is a cyclical process of assessing performance, implementing changes, and evaluating results. The Plan-Do-Study-Act (PDSA) cycle (Deming, 1986) is a widely used model:

- **Plan**: Identify an opportunity and plan a change.
- **Do**: Test the change on a small scale.
- **Study**: Review and analyze the results.
- **Act**: Implement the change on a larger scale if successful, or refine and retest.

Data-driven decision-making improves program effectiveness, fosters accountability, and builds credibility with stakeholders.

Build It: Step-by-Step

Step 1: Define key performance indicators (KPIs) aligned with your program goals.
Step 2: Collect data systematically and consistently.
Step 3: Review data regularly in team meetings.
Step 4: Use findings to make targeted improvements.
Step 5: Share successes and lessons learned with stakeholders.
Step 6: Repeat the cycle for ongoing improvement.

Practice Lab

- **Reflection**: How is your program currently using data?
- **Prompt**: Which metrics truly reflect the impact you want to have?
- **Exercise**: Identify one process or outcome to monitor using the PDSA cycle.
- **Application**: Implement one data-informed change within the next 30 days.

4-Layer Integration

1. **Conscious**: Clear metrics and data collection plan.
2. **Pre-conscious**: Awareness of patterns emerging from data.
3. **Unconscious**: Habit of data-informed thinking.
4. **Existential**: Commitment to truth and transparency for better outcomes.

References

Deming, W. E. (1986). *Out of the crisis*. MIT Press

Chapter 45: Strategic Partnerships for Power, Reach & Sustainability

When the Safe Steps Initiative began offering services to survivors of domestic violence, demand quickly outpaced capacity. Instead of trying to meet every need alone, the leadership formed strategic partnerships with housing agencies, legal aid organizations, and local healthcare providers. By working together, they created a seamless referral network that expanded access, reduced duplication, and provided holistic support to participants.

Conversation

Karen: *'You can't do everything alone—and you shouldn't try.'*

Mardoche: *'Partnerships can multiply your impact without multiplying your costs.'*

Luis: *'But they need to be intentional, not just a handshake.'*

Amira: *'The best partnerships are mutually beneficial and built on trust.'*

Science Break

Strategic partnerships are formal or informal collaborations between organizations that share resources, expertise, and responsibilities to achieve common goals. According to Austin and Seitanidi's Collaboration Continuum (2012), partnerships can progress through stages:

- **Philanthropic**: One organization provides resources to another.
- **Transactional**: Organizations exchange resources or services.
- **Integrative**: Partners align strategies and share decision-making.
- **Transformational**: Partnerships create systemic change beyond individual organizations.

Build It: Step-by-Step

Step 1: Identify gaps your organization cannot fill alone.
Step 2: Map potential partners with aligned missions.
Step 3: Initiate conversations to explore mutual benefits.
Step 4: Formalize agreements (e.g., MOUs, contracts) where needed.
Step 5: Establish clear communication and accountability structures.
Step 6: Review and adjust partnerships periodically.

Practice Lab

- **Reflection**: Who could you partner with to expand your program's reach or effectiveness?
- **Prompt**: What would a truly mutually beneficial partnership look like in your context?
- **Exercise**: Create a partner mapping diagram showing current and potential collaborators.
- **Application**: Reach out to one potential partner this month to explore collaboration.

4-Layer Integration

1. **Conscious**: List of potential and current partners.
2. **Pre-conscious**: Awareness of shared goals and values.
3. **Unconscious**: Habit of seeking collaboration over competition.
4. **Existential**: Commitment to collective impact.

References

Austin, J. E., & Seitanidi, M. M. (2012). Collaborative value creation: A review of partnering between nonprofits and businesses. *Nonprofit and Voluntary Sector Quarterly, 41*(5), 726–758.

Chapter 46: Sustainability from Day One: Building Programs that Endure

The Fresh Path Community Health Project launched with a large grant and ambitious goals. However, as the grant's end date approached, staff realized they had no plan for how to maintain services. Programs began to wind down, and community members felt abandoned. In contrast, a neighboring program, launched at the same time, built sustainability into its plan from day one, diversifying funding, building community ownership, and integrating services into existing systems. Ten years later, it's still thriving.

Conversation

Karen: *'Sustainability doesn't start when the money runs out. It starts before the program begins.'*

Mardoche: *'Think of it like planting a tree. You plan for it to grow long after you're gone.'*

Luis: *'It's about more than money. It's about structures, people, and commitment.'*

Amira: *'And making the program indispensable to the community.'*

Science Break

Sustainability planning involves ensuring that a program's benefits continue over time, even if initial funding or leadership changes. According to the Program Sustainability Assessment Tool (Luke et al., 2014), sustainable programs:

- Have a clear mission and demonstrated impact.
- Diversify funding sources.
- Build strong community partnerships.
- Integrate into existing systems and policies.
- Develop leadership and staff capacity.
- Continuously adapt based on feedback and evaluation.

Build It: Step-by-Step

Step 1: Define your sustainability vision and goals.
Step 2: Identify and diversify funding streams.
Step 3: Build strong relationships with stakeholders.
Step 4: Integrate services into existing community systems.
Step 5: Develop leadership succession and capacity-building plans.
Step 6: Monitor and adjust sustainability strategies over time.

Practice Lab

- **Reflection**: What would it take for your program to thrive for 10+ years?
- **Prompt**: Which funding or structural vulnerabilities exist in your current model?
- **Exercise**: Create a sustainability map that includes funding, partnerships, and integration points.
- **Application**: Implement one sustainability-enhancing strategy within the next quarter.

4-Layer Integration

1. **Conscious**: Written sustainability plan.
2. **Pre-conscious**: Awareness of long-term needs and vulnerabilities.
3. **Unconscious**: Habit of planning for continuity.
4. **Existential**: Commitment to leaving a lasting impact.

References

Luke, D. A., Calhoun, A., Robichaux, C. B., Elliott, M. B., & Moreland-Russell, S. (2014). The Program Sustainability Assessment Tool: A new instrument for public health programs. *Preventing Chronic Disease, 11*, E12.

Part VI — The Future of Program Design

Chapter 47: The Future of Program Design: AI, Integration & Human-Centered Systems

In 2035, the Sunrise Behavioral Health Network operates in ways unimaginable two decades earlier. AI-driven analytics anticipate community needs before they arise, virtual reality tools simulate coping strategies for clients, and every program is co-created with real-time community feedback. This transformation began in 2025, when leaders committed to reimagining program design for an uncertain future—one shaped by rapid technological innovation, shifting demographics, and new understandings of mental health and wellness.

Conversation

Karen: *'The pace of change is only accelerating. Our programs have to be ready for what's next.'*

Mardoche: *'Future-ready design means building adaptability into the DNA of our programs.'*

Luis: *'Technology is a tool, but people remain at the center.'*

Amira: *'The future belongs to those who can learn, unlearn, and relearn.'*

Science Break

The future of program design will be influenced by trends in technology, population health, social policy, and climate change (World Health Organization, 2021). Effective programs will integrate predictive analytics, person-centered approaches, and sustainable practices to remain relevant and impactful.

Emerging drivers of program design:

- Predictive and prescriptive analytics.
- Integration of digital and in-person services.
- Cross-sector collaborations.
- Focus on prevention and upstream interventions.
- Climate resilience and environmental sustainability.

Build It: Step-by-Step

Step 1: Conduct regular environmental scans for emerging trends.
Step 2: Invest in adaptable infrastructure.
Step 3: Develop continuous learning systems for staff.
Step 4: Pilot innovative approaches in low-risk settings.
Step 5: Engage diverse voices to anticipate future needs.
Step 6: Integrate sustainability into every aspect of program design.

Practice Lab

- **Reflection**: What trends could most impact your program in the next 10 years?
- **Prompt**: How can you build flexibility into your current program structures?
- **Exercise**: Create a 'future scenarios' plan with at least three possible futures.
- **Application**: Test one future-focused idea in a small pilot project.

4-Layer Integration

1. **Conscious**: Regularly updated strategic plan informed by trend analysis.
2. **Pre-conscious**: Organizational habits of scanning and adapting.
3. **Unconscious**: Comfort with uncertainty and change.
4. **Existential**: Commitment to shaping the future in alignment with core values.

References

World Health Organization. (2021). *Global report on health futures*. WHO Press.

Chapter 48: Lessons from the Field: Wisdom from Clinicians & Leaders

Over the past decade, the Community Resilience Collaborative (CRC) implemented programs across urban, rural, and international settings. Their successes and failures offer invaluable lessons. In one rural county, a mobile mental health unit flourished by leveraging trusted community leaders. In an urban setting, a similar model faltered due to insufficient engagement with local grassroots organizations. CRC learned that context, culture, and collaboration are as critical as funding and staffing.

Conversation

Karen: *'The field teaches us things textbooks can't.'*

Mardoche: *'Our best teacher is reflection on our own work.'*

Luis: *'We can learn as much from missteps as from wins.'*

Amira: *'And sharing those lessons openly strengthens the whole sector.'*

Science Break

Practice-based evidence complements evidence-based practice by drawing from real-world implementation experiences (Green, Glasgow, & Atkins, 2009). Documenting and disseminating lessons learned improves collective knowledge, informs adaptations, and reduces the likelihood of repeating avoidable mistakes.

Key strategies for capturing lessons from the field:

- Structured reflection sessions.
- Stakeholder debriefs and focus groups.
- Continuous quality improvement cycles.
- Peer-to-peer learning networks.

Build It: Step-by-Step

Step 1: Establish mechanisms to capture lessons throughout program implementation.
Step 2: Document both successes and challenges.
Step 3: Share findings internally and externally.
Step 4: Integrate lessons into future program planning.
Step 5: Create a culture of openness and learning.

Practice Lab

- **Reflection**: What lessons have emerged from your program's journey so far?
- **Prompt**: Which challenges provided the richest learning?
- **Exercise**: Conduct a 'lessons learned' workshop with your team.
- **Application**: Apply one insight from the past year to a current program decision.

4-Layer Integration

1. **Conscious**: Written lessons learned report.
2. **Pre-conscious**: Habit of documenting and discussing field experiences.
3. **Unconscious**: Valuing vulnerability as a path to growth.
4. **Existential**: Recognizing that every experience—good or bad—advances the mission.

References

Green, L. W., Glasgow, R. E., & Atkins, D. (2009). Making evidence from research more relevant, useful, and actionable in policy, program planning, and practice: Slips 'twixt cup and lip. *American Journal of Preventive Medicine, 37*(6 Suppl. 1), S187–S191.

Chapter 49: The New Architecture of Care — From Services → Systems → Ecosystems

When the Horizon Multi-Agency Collaborative first formed, it wasn't meant to be a revolution. It was simply a group of clinicians, outreach workers, school leaders, housing partners, and community elders meeting in a church basement to discuss the same families they all kept seeing. One resident, a grandmother caring for three grandchildren, had four case managers, two care coordinators, and five different appointments per week.

She said, *'I feel like the whole city is helping me, but none of you are talking to each other.'*

That moment changed everything. The group decided to stop operating as disconnected services and instead began designing a shared system. They created a unified engagement pathway, co-located teams, integrated data dashboards, and a community advisory council. Within a year, duplication dropped by 40%, residents reported higher satisfaction, hospitalizations decreased, and the grandmother said, *'Now it feels like one team.'*

Conversation

Karen: *'People don't need more services. They need systems that make sense.'*

Mardoche: *'And systems don't need to be complicated. They need to be connected.'*

Luis: *'The mistake is thinking of programs as islands.'*

Amira: *'The future is ecosystem design—interlocking solutions that strengthen each other.'*

Science Break

Ecosystem thinking in mental health and social services draws from systems science, ecology, and complexity theory. Research shows that interconnected systems, where information, resources, and relationships flow freely, produce more stable, resilient, and high-impact outcomes (Meadows, 2008).

Three Levels of the Care Ecosystem:

1. **Services**: Individual programs with limited scope and reach.
2. **Systems**: Coordinated networks across sectors (education, housing, health, justice).
3. **Ecosystems**: Fully integrated environments where policies, practices, and partnerships reinforce one another.

Across industries, ecosystem-based approaches outperform linear service models in both efficiency and outcomes (Holling, 2001).

Build It: Step-by-Step — Designing Ecosystems of Care

Step 1: Map what already exists. Identify services, partners, gaps, duplications, and natural strengths.

Step 2: Define shared goals. A system only forms when all actors move toward a single north star.

Step 3: Build shared pathways. Unify engagement, referral, crisis, and follow-up processes across organizations.

Step 4: Integrate communication. Cross-sector huddles, universal scripts, shared dashboards, and multi-team rounds.

Step 5: Establish feedback loops. Real-time data, community feedback, and continuous improvement cycles.

Step 6: Transfer ownership. Communities must eventually shape and lead the ecosystem for long-term transformation.

Practice Lab

- **Reflection**: Where does fragmentation still exist in your system?
- **Prompt**: Who else should be 'in the room' that isn't currently at the table?
- **Exercise**: Create a visual ecosystem map of your community—services, systems, influences.

- **Application**: Initiate a cross-sector ecosystem meeting within the next 30 days.

4-Layer Integration

1. **Conscious**: Clear system maps, shared workflows, and written agreements.
2. **Pre-conscious**: Habitual collaboration and automatic communication channels.
3. **Unconscious**: A culture that assumes partnership as the default.
4. **Existential**: A community that sees itself as one integrated organism working for collective well-being.

References

- Holling, C. S. (2001). Understanding the complexity of economic, ecological, and social systems. *Ecosystems, 4*(5), 390–405.
- Meadows, D. H. (2008). *Thinking in systems: A primer*. Chelsea Green Publishing.

Conclusion

The Work Begins Now

At the beginning of this book, there was a person, sitting in a room, surrounded by services, yet disconnected from care. Nothing about that moment was rare. It happens every day across systems, whether health, housing, justice, or education. People labeled "non-compliant" are often navigating fragmentation; and now, you see it. You see the gaps, the misalignment, and the missed opportunities; and once you see it, you cannot unsee it. As such, this is the turning point. You are not just working in a system. You are shaping it, as the system itself is part of the intervention.

This book gave you tools, but tools alone don't change systems. Action does. Systems change when people build differently. You don't need to redesign everything. Start with one program, one workflow, one team. Ask: What is not aligned? Where are people falling through? What can be simplified? Close one gap; and then another; and then another, for systems are living. They evolve; and this work is never finished.

As such, it is not about perfection. It is about alignment, responsiveness, and humanity; and every decision matters, as systems are built through repeated actions over time.

Return to that person. What would change if the system worked? This book is an invitation to not simply understand, but to build, for the system is not something you work in. It is something you are responsible for shaping; and if people are still falling through the cracks, which means the work is not finished, though the goal was never to do more; rather, it was always to build something that works. In this vein, now, the work begins.

Invitation to the Reader

From Insight to Action

You have reached the end of this book, but not the end of the work.

If you've made it this far, something has already shifted. You've seen the gaps, the misalignment, and the patterns that shape systems. You now have a choice.

Consider pausing before you move on, and ask yourself the following: What did I see differently? What made me uncomfortable? What have I been tolerating? What is one thing I will change?

Whether it is one program, or one workflow, or one meeting, or one expectation, just act, without waiting to have it figured out perfectly. Just be intentional; and for this, consider the following 7-Day Commitment: Within the next 7 days, implement one real change:

- Redesign a workflow
- Clarify a process
- Initiate a cross-team conversation
- Implement one metric
- Address one engagement barrier

Moreover, remember you are not alone in this work. Build with others and learn together, for systems change collectively. In this spirit, if this book moved you, share it so others can begin building systems that work, while helping each other remember that we don't need more time. We don't need more permission. We need one decision: to stop adapting to systems that don't work and start building ones that do.

Appendix

Tools for Building Programs That Work

How to Use This Appendix

This section is designed to move you from understanding to implementation. Use these tools individually, within a team, or as part of a full program rollout. Start with one.

Appendix A: The One-Page Program Design Template

Program Name:

Population Served:

Problem Being Addressed:

Core Intervention:

Workflow:

1.

2.

3.

4.

Team Roles:

Expected Outcomes:

Appendix B: The First 90 Days Implementation Plan

Phase 1 (Days 1–30): Clarity

- Define program
- Identify team
- Create workflow
- Assign owner

Phase 2 (Days 31–60): Consistency

- Run weekly
- Standardize language
- Track engagement

Phase 3 (Days 61–90): Stabilization

- Fix breakdowns
- Clarify roles
- Build routine

Appendix C: Engagement Script Toolkit

- First Contact: What would make this worth your time today?
- Validation: That makes sense given what you're dealing with.
- Follow-Up: We missed you. Please tell us what happened.

Appendix D: Team Check-In Framework

1. What's working?
2. What's not?
3. What's unclear?
4. What feels heavy?

Appendix E: Funding Map Template

Activity	Funding Source	Gap

Appendix F: Metrics Dashboard

- Behavioral: follow-up within 48 hrs
- Process: sessions completed
- Outcome: reduced ER visits

Appendix G: Equity Audit Tool

- Who is served?
- Who is not?
- Where is drop-off?
- What barriers exist?

Appendix H: System Integration Map

List systems:

- Health
- Housing
- Justice
- Education

Identify connections and gaps

Appendix I: 7-Day Action Plan

- Day 1–2: Identify gap
- Day 3–4: Design change
- Day 5–6: Implement
- Day 7: Review

Appendix J: SWEET 4-Layer Reflection Tool

- Conscious: What is happening?
- Pre-conscious: Patterns?
- Unconscious: Drivers?
- Existential: Meaning?

Start small. Stay consistent. Build something that works.

Appendix K

Implementation Playbook - From Reading to Building

How to Use This Playbook

This playbook helps you move from insight to implementation. Start with one action.

Where to Start (Choose Your Role)

- Clinician: Focus on engagement and follow-up.
- Program Director: Focus on workflow and metrics.
- Leader: Focus on alignment and sustainability.
- Team: Use tools together.

30-Day Implementation Path

- Week 1: Clarity – define program
- Week 2: Engagement – improve entry and retention
- Week 3: Team Alignment – simplify and align
- Week 4: Metrics + Sustainability – track and adjust

Core Tools

- Program Design Template
- First 90 Days Plan
- Engagement Scripts
- Team Check-In
- Metrics Dashboard
- Equity Audit

Team Implementation Model

- Start small → Build rhythm → Learn fast → Expand

Integration Across Systems

- Identify systems, gaps, and initiate one coordinated meeting.

Equity in Action

- Identify one inequity and implement one structural change.

Metrics That Drive Behavior

- Choose 3–5 metrics. Review weekly. Adjust continuously.

Continuous Improvement Loop

- What worked?
- What didn't?
- What will change?

Common Mistakes to Avoid

- Doing too much
- Overcomplicating
- Ignoring team dynamics
- Measuring everything
- Waiting for perfect

Your Commitment

System to improve:

First change:

Next step (7 days):

Start. Adjust. Build something that works.

Recommended Reading

Deepening the Work

This book is not an endpoint. It is an entry point.

The following readings are curated to deepen your understanding and expand your ability to design systems that work.

1. Systems Thinking & Design

- Meadows, D. H. (2008). *Thinking in systems: A primer*. Chelsea Green Publishing.
- Senge, P. M. (2006). *The fifth discipline: The art and practice of the learning organization* (Rev. and updated ed.). Doubleday.
- Liedtka, J., & Ogilvie, T. (2011). *Designing for growth: A design thinking tool kit for managers*. Columbia University Press.

2. Implementation Science & Change

- Fixsen, D. L., Naoom, S. F., Blase, K. A., Friedman, R. M., & Wallace, F. (2005). *Implementation research: A synthesis of the literature*. University of South Florida, Louis de la Parte Florida Mental Health Institute.
- Heath, C., & Heath, D. (2010). *Switch: How to change things when change is hard*. Broadway Books.
- Langley, G. J., Moen, R. D., Nolan, K. M., Nolan, T. W., Norman, C. L., & Provost, L. P. (2009). *The improvement guide: A practical approach to enhancing organizational performance* (2nd ed.). Jossey-Bass.

3. Mental Health & Human Behavior

- van der Kolk, B. A. (2014). The body keeps the score: Brain, mind, and body in the healing of trauma. Viking.

- Frankl, V. E. (2006). Man's search for meaning. Beacon Press.
- Miller, W. R., & Rollnick, S. (2013). Motivational interviewing: Helping people change (3rd ed.). Guilford Press.

4. Leadership & Organizational Change

- Collins, J. (2001). Good to great: Why some companies make the leap...and others don't. HarperBusiness.
- Sinek, S. (2014). Leaders eat last: Why some teams pull together and others don't. Portfolio/Penguin.
- Marquet, L. D. (2013). Turn the ship around!: A true story of turning followers into leaders. Portfolio/Penguin.

5. Equity, Ethics, and Social Justice

- Washington, H. A. (2006). Medical apartheid: The dark history of medical experimentation on Black Americans from colonial times to the present. Doubleday.
- Stevenson, B. (2015). Just mercy: A story of justice and redemption. Spiegel & Grau.
- Farmer, P. (2003). Pathologies of power: Health, human rights, and the new war on the poor. University of California Press.

Reminder: The goal is not to know more. The goal is to build better.

About the Authors

Mardoche Sidor, MD

Mardoche Sidor, MD is a quadruple board-certified psychiatrist in General Psychiatry, Child and Adolescent Psychiatry, Forensic Psychiatry, and Addiction Psychiatry. He is also formally trained in Public and Community Psychiatry, Geriatric Psychiatry, and multiple evidence-based and psychodynamic treatment modalities.

Dr. Sidor is the Founder of the SWEET Institute, a global learning and practice community dedicated to transforming how mental health, human development, and systems of care are understood and implemented. He currently serves as Chief Medical Officer at Urban Pathways in New York City, where he leads system-level initiatives to improve care for individuals experiencing homelessness, serious mental illness, substance use challenges, and complex health and social needs.

He is a candidate at the Columbia University Center for Psychoanalytic Training and Research and previously served as Assistant Clinical Professor of Psychiatry at Columbia University Vagelos College of Physicians and Surgeons. His work integrates neuroscience, psychoanalysis, cognitive and behavioral approaches, and systems design to bridge the gap between knowledge and sustainable implementation.

Dr. Sidor's work focuses on a central question:

How do we move from understanding to lasting change, at the level of individuals, teams, and systems?

Karen Dubin, PhD, LCSW

Karen Dubin, PhD, LCSW is a clinical social worker, educator, and leader with extensive experience in psychotherapy, supervision, and professional training. She has played a central role in shaping the SWEET Institute's clinical and educational frameworks, helping translate complex psychological theories into practical, accessible tools for clinicians and organizations.

Dr. Dubin brings expertise in psychodynamic therapy, relational approaches, and clinical supervision, combined with a commitment to experiential learning and professional growth. Her work emphasizes the integration of theory and practice.

She has been instrumental in co-developing SWEET Institute's training programs, publications, and community-based learning models, contributing to a growing body of work focused on transformation across clinical, organizational, and systemic levels.

Her work centers on a guiding principle:

Real change happens when knowledge becomes lived experience.

The SWEET Institute

The SWEET Institute is a global learning and practice community dedicated to advancing mental health, human development, and system transformation.

Through courses, trainings, publications, and community engagement, the Institute focuses on bridging the gap between knowledge and implementation, theory and practice, and insight and sustainable change.

The SWEET Institute is grounded in a central belief:

Transformation happens when individuals and systems move through the four layers of change: conscious, pre-conscious, unconscious, and existential, and integrate learning into consistent action.

Through its work, the SWEET Institute supports clinicians, leaders, and organizations in building programs that work, improving engagement and outcomes, creating sustainable systems of care, and fostering alignment across teams and structures.

This book reflects not only the work of its authors, but the collective learning of clinicians, leaders, and communities committed to building systems that work.

www.ingramcontent.com/pod-product-compliance
Lightning Source LLC
Chambersburg PA
CBHW041258210926
51847CB00009B/68
* 9 7 8 1 9 6 8 1 0 5 4 6 4 *